The Miracle of Recovery

Sharon Wegscheider-Cruse

Health Communications, Inc.
Deerfield Beach, Florida

Sharon Wegscheider-Cruse
ONSITE Training & Consulting, Inc.
2820 West Main
Rapid City, SD 57702

Library of Congress Cataloging-in-Publication Data

Wegscheider-Cruse, Sharon
    The miracle of recovery: healing for addicts, adult children,
and co-dependents.

    Bibliography: p.
    1. Compulsive behavior.   2. Adult children of
alcoholics.   3. Co-dependence (Psychology)   I. Title.
RC533.W44   1989   616.86   88-34770
ISBN 1-55874-024-4

©1989 Sharon Wegscheider-Cruse
ISBN 1-55874-024-4

Published by: Health Communications, Inc.
                3201 S.W. 15th Street
                Deerfield Beach, Florida 33442

DEDICATION

... to all people who have been supportive and caring of me, "my angels" . . . .

... to my children and their mates who have loved me always and allow me to love them . . . .

... to the Onsite staff who have taught me the value of teamwork . . . .

... to our "group leader teams," my family of choice who share the Recovery spiritual journey . . . .

... to my partner Joe, my soulmate who shares my every moment . . . .

... to myself, in appreciation for the courage to make the choices I have . . . .

... most especially — to my Higher Power for directing my life better than I ever could . . . .

A special thank you to Kathleen Johnson for her hours of work on the manuscript and creative talent of the drawings and cover design.

The Miracle of Recovery is a book born out of the need to express the idea of wholeness and the vision of healing. So often we complicate our recovery by dwelling in the drama of describing and reiterating sickness. It is a refreshing change to see a book dedicated solely to the unlimited potential that exists in us all.

In a clean, concise manner, Sharon describes the journey from the darkness of addictive behavior into the dawn of freedom. I recommend *The Miracle of Recovery* to all who are interested in healing and transformation.

Rokelle Lerner

CONTENTS

FOREWORD

I have not checked with the record, but I believe it would be safe to bet that no Vince Lombardi Green Bay Packer team ever lost two games in a row. When on extremely rare occasions one of his teams lost a game, Mr. Lombardi spent the next practice sessions drilling his players in the ABCs of the game — blocking and tackling. And God help next Sunday's opponent.

Sharon Wegscheider-Cruse has been for years a true pioneer who has blazed many new trails in pursuit of health and happiness for families plagued by addiction. She has been eminently successful. I believe that the main reason is that she has never forgotten to emphasize the basics of general wellness — the principles of AA.

Some years ago I was able to share with her Dr. Bob Smith's magnificent six-word summary of the AA Steps — "Trust God. Clean House. Help Others." She said the brilliance and simplicity of his formula for good health affected her profoundly. This shows not only in her work, but in her written works, especially her newest, *The Miracle of Recovery*.

In an era of new movements, many of them good and effective, an era of buzz words and phrases of the month, Sharon Wegscheider-Cruse stands out as one who has never forgotten basics, who constantly emphasizes the goal above all — getting well. Many people yearn to explore the past, finding out the *whys* of their illness and in the doing, forget the *how* to seek wellness. Intrigued by how sick they got, they bounce from one workshop to another. Many unconsciously feel that they can absorb in two days what the presenter has taken a lifetime to acquire. We must never forget that a little knowledge is a very dangerous thing indeed.

If you want to know Sharon Wegscheider-Cruse, read *The Miracle of Recovery* and you will find out why she stands so tall, not only in the field of addiction, but in our hearts.

Father Martin

Dear Reader:

Every year as I have met many, many people in either a counseling, training or a teaching setting, I have been surprised, awed and respectful of the difficult situations that people have lived through and yet have continued to grow in their own recovery against sometimes the most painful odds. I have said to myself, and often I've overheard at meetings and different settings, "What a miracle!" "It's just a miracle that this has happened." I've heard counselors say, "I've watched miracles consistently in treatment." In 12-step programs I have listened to people talk about the many miracles that they have witnessed.

My own recovery is one such miracle. This word became such an important one to me that one day I went to the dictionary for a definition. Webster defines a miracle as *"An event that appears unexplainable by laws of nature and so is held to be an Act of God."*

A miracle is "An event that appears unexplainable by laws of nature and so is held to be an Act of God."

I feel that for me. I feel that I am a very ordinary woman who lives a very extraordinary life. How did a little girl from a family of very simple means with generations of alcoholism ever arrive at a lifestyle of joy, comfort, fulfillment, intimacy, family, friends and a sense of meaning? It can only be called a miracle. As I felt the truth of the word, I began to understand.

There is the possibility of taking a complete look at one's history and beginning to reframe life experience to see how a miracle has unfolded. At this point when I look at my own life, I can see clearly there was a pattern of behavior that I repeated many times. The more I learned to recognize the pattern, the more I began to trust and to heal. In studying my own life I found there were actually stages of healing. I'm going to identify in this book the stages of healing that I have only been able to recognize and understand when looking backwards. I certainly did not plan to go through them.

I once heard somebody say in one of our programs, *"True spirituality is living life forward but understanding it backward."*

---•---

*"True spirituality is living life forward
but understanding it backward."*

---•---

Today I know what this statement means. I can see that so often in my life I groped and I tried and I made efforts and I had plans and I organized. I'm a busy kind of a person. And so often my plans were changed outside myself. My organizing didn't work. Barriers were given to me. Roadblocks were set up. I was forced to go another way by circumstances of the reality that I was in. Today as I look backwards, I can see that the journey went just the way it needed to go. I love where I'm at today, even though I got there in spite of myself. An anonymous prayer that my husband, Joe Cruse, found in a treatment center tells my story better than I, and I would like to share this with you.

TODAY

I asked God for strength that I might achieve;
I was made weak that I might humbly learn to obey.

I asked for help that I might do great things;
I was given infirmity that I might do better things.

I asked for riches that I might be happy;
I was given poverty that I might be wise.

I asked for power that I might have the praise of men;
I was given weakness that I might feel the need of God.

I asked for all things that I might enjoy life;
I was given life that I might enjoy all things.

I asked for a vision that I might control my future;
I was given awareness that I might be grateful now.

I got nothing I asked for but everything I had hoped for.
Almost in spite of myself my unspoken prayers were answered.

I am among all people most richly blessed.

For myself, I'm totally satisfied believing in the miracle of "me." I'm excited and grateful, and I'd like to share some of my thoughts with you.

Many clients have come to our programs in a hectic spiritual quest, so busy learning, exploring and experiencing that they have missed the miracle that has already taken place. They have missed the miracle of themselves. They are tired and desperately searching. I offer this book to them and to you, in gratitude of the miracle of "me" and in hope that you recognize the miracle of "you."

To recognize the miracle of you means that some begin and others continue to recognize their own journey of recovery from a painful family system and relationships. It is to move from being simply a survivor of historical pain to becoming a celebrator who knows what recovery and inner peace are all about. It is to really accept a personal transformation and a celebration of a true recovery. I hope that the things I share in this book will be "Good News."

It's been wonderful these past few years as we have been learning about the mystery of co-dependency and the lives of adult children or grandchildren from alcoholic or painful homes. Knowledge has helped many to identify and understand what has happened to them as children. The good news is that many have sought professional care and many more have made healthy choices in their day-to-day living and are living lives that are rich and satisfying. Others, however, have stayed stuck in the problem identification and often feel more frustrated than they did before they started learning.

This book is about the "Good News." It is meant to offer the possibility of another look at history and the possibility of reframing our life experience to take a bigger and more complete look at our experiences.

This book is about the "Good News."

Sharon

Part One
Recognition of
a Miracle

1

Reframe Thinking

There are two forms of denial that adult children often experience. One is the denial of the reality of what was: minimizing and distorting the painful experiences in order to survive. Much has already been written about the painful denial. The second form of denial is the denial of hope and possibility, the reality of what could be.

Because our past experiences have been full of pain and dysfunction, we find it difficult to believe our future does not have to be the same way. We need to learn to break out of that pattern of thinking. We can begin to recognize the positive elements of our past as well as the negative painful elements. We can reframe our thinking to see the strengths we have gained from our experiences.

2

Divine Protection

One way to begin to reinterpret experiences is to go back and look for the signs of *Divine Protection* in one's life. Divine Protection is what has taken care of you in years past.

---

*One way to begin to reinterpret experiences
is to go back and look for the signs of
Divine Protection in one's life.*

Some of my favorite "Divine Protection" memories:

Florida Trips

When I was a little girl, my family would take vacation trips to Florida. Before we left our small Minnesota town on an old two-lane highway, my dad would stop at his business place and pick up a six pack of Coca-Cola and another of Orange Crush. My brother, sister and I would "drink the tops off" the bottles of soda. For us that meant drinking the top half of the bottle. My dad would then fill up the Coke bottles with rum for himself and the Orange Crush with vodka for my mom. We'd take off at 85 miles per hour all the way to Florida.

We drove straight through, stopping only for gas, soda, food and liquor. Never once did we encounter an accident. Never once did we cause one. Two intoxicated drivers going clear across the country at unlawful speeds — what Divine Protection we must have had.

Flat Tire

One hot summer night I was coming home from a teaching class at the University of Minnesota about 10:30 p.m. I was tired and decided to take a short cut through a part of town known for its high crime rate. About half way through this fairly dangerous section one of the tires on my car blew. Before long I could feel the rim of the wheel clanking on the highway. It was clear I was not going to be able to go on. I got out of the car and walked, and I was very frightened.

After a couple of dark blocks, I saw a faint light coming from the porch of a large house. Gathering my courage, I headed for the porch. Looking inside a screened porch door, I saw a group of tough-looking men. My first instinct was to run. Yet where? Finally I knocked. A burly man came to the door. As I was telling him my plight, he interrupted by asking, "Are you the alcohol lady?" He then produced one of my books with my picture on it. I had interrupted a local AA meeting.

The whole group trudged down the hill, fixed my tire, shared the serenity prayer with me and I was on my way.

Red Rose Of Texas

After years of personal and professional life in Minnesota, it seemed clear to me that it was time for a change. Several circumstances told me it was time to leave in the winter of 1982-83. With the offer of a meaningful job in Texas, I sold my home, left my family, friends and career. I headed for Texas on a cold December day.

I was driving a small grey Honda and was dressed warmly in a grey snowsuit with a red knit hat and red down-lined cowboy boots. A few hours into the three-day drive I was battling a snowstorm. By the time I neared the Texas border after two days of treacherous ice-driving, my emotions were tense and vulnerable. I was feeling personally alone and totally non-cared-for. I also felt professionally isolated from friends and peers. The tears began to flow. After about two hours of crying and driving, I prayed.

"Dear God, I feel so alone and so unsure. If I have anyone who cares, personally or professionally, please give me a sign." I continued to drive. Shortly after I saw a roadside diner and decided to stop and take a break.

As I entered the restaurant, I picked up a magazine to read. I sat down in a booth and the waitress came over. The first thing she said was, "You must be Red Rose." Puzzled, I asked her to explain. She said, "The truck drivers are all talking about the red rose. Some lady left Minnesota in a small grey Honda in the middle of a snowstorm and they've been concerned and watching out for her from Minnesota to the Texas border. They've followed her on their C.B.s to make sure she was okay. I see you've made it, and I'll let them know."

My tears began to flow again, this time from relief and gratitude. I felt watched over and protected. The sign had been given to me. Personally, I was being cared for.

As I began to eat my sandwich and sip coffee, I opened the magazine. The article I was drawn to said *"Families of Alcoholics Recover."* The article began "Sharon Wegscheider, in her work, reports, etc. etc." I could not remember giving an interview to this particular magazine and yet here was an article about my work. Even professionally I felt protected. Divinely protected. The tears were replaced by a smile.

Divine Protection has probably also worked in your life many times. In addition to the Higher Power giving divine protection, God has always answered prayers by sending people. These people I call "Angels."

3

Angels

My very special grandma was an angel to me. I can still hear her voice saying, "I love you just the way you are." Two of my aunts were there for me when I needed parenting. My high school speech coach prepared me for a future I didn't understand. It makes perfect sense to me today that she pushed me in speech and communication classes.

Angels come in two styles, Mentors and Teachers.

Mentors are those who show us the way, support us and share their wisdom. My Higher Power sent me several: my Aunt Elaine, who taught me about my femininity, Eugene Burke, who taught me about true spirituality and Virginia Satir, who taught me about choice.

Teachers are those from whom we learn lessons (sometimes the hard way). One of my teachers was an arrogant and sexist person in authority at one of my jobs. When my suffering in working at his agency got too great, I wanted to leave that job. He taught me the value of my own well-being and forced me to learn about risk-taking. My Higher Power sent just the right angel at just the right time.

One good friend stood by and supported me in all my changes, even when he didn't understand. There was also a counselor who believed in me before I believed in myself. Today I recognize these special angels my Higher Power (who I choose to call "God") sent to me to keep me protected and on my survival path.

If the Higher Power and special angels felt I was worth it, I have accepted that I can do no less. Today I am filled with love and compassion for the little girl inside me who struggled and made it. I have made a commitment to her not to leave her in confusion, fear or mistrust. I commit to do whatever is necessary for her to be safe, healthy and free.

The old definition of trust is that I had to learn to trust others. That way I had to wait for others to change and prove themselves. The new definition of trust is that I have to trust myself. Today I trust myself to make the most of what I have, learn gratitude for how far I've come and set the necessary boundaries that keep me safe.

---

*Today I trust myself to make the most of
what I have, learn gratitude for how far I've
come and set the necessary boundaries
that keep me safe.*

I give myself permission to claim my worthiness. If my Higher Power saw to it that I made it this far, the least I can do is take it from here. If my Higher Power thinks I'm worth it, how can I appreciate myself any less?

The realist knows that the child from a painful family is, in many ways, a gifted child. From *Business Week* (September 30, 1985):

> Creative types are generally independent and highly motivated. They are also great skeptics, risk-takers and thinkers. Disorder doesn't make them anxious. Indeed, they relish it.
>
> "Creative people usually don't have dull, predictable childhoods. Instead, childhood is marked by 'Exposure To Diversity'," says Dean K. Simonton, a psychologist at the University of California-Davis. Strains in family life, financial ups and downs or divorces are common. Experts believe a dose of adversity gives children the ability to see issues and problems from different points of view.

4

Lost And Found Department

Looking back on my life, I devised a framework I call The Lost and Found Department. After grieving my losses, I began to take a closer look and have begun to understand their importance in my life.

Lost	Found
1. My father at an early age.	Confidence to care for myself.
2. Friends when I divorced.	New relationships.
3. My ability to be strong.	The ability to accept support.
4. Friends to addiction and co-dependency.	Ability to set boundaries for myself.
5. My job because of my convictions.	A whole new field to work in with the best professionals in the field.

With the proven history of divine protection and the obvious presence of angels in my past, it is easy to give myself permission to believe in miracles and proclaim myself a realist. The reality is clear. Today I understand the chaos of the past. Everything has happened as it needed to. I trust it will continue to do so.

With the proven history of Divine Protection and the obvious presence of angels in my past, it is easy to give myself permission to believe in miracles and proclaim myself a realist.

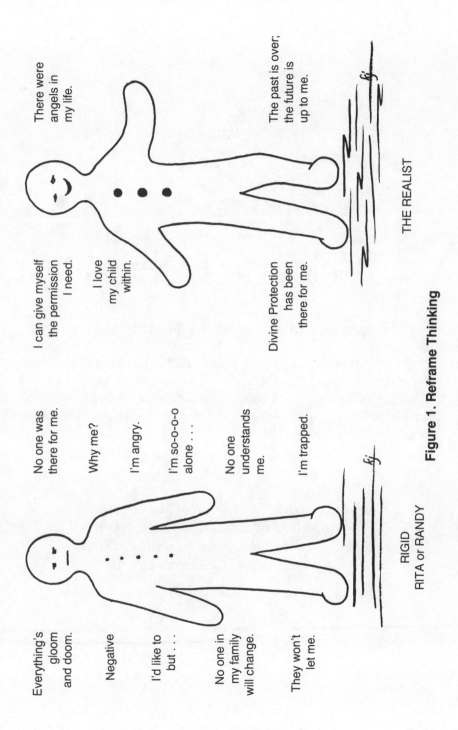

Figure 1. Reframe Thinking

5

Welcome Feelings

✓ My job is to take necessary action in order to pick up on the clues of where my journey is taking me. Basically, I love to learn, explore and study. Like many other adult children and co-dependents, I have been consuming information for many years. But there comes a time when learning is not enough. At that moment it's time to stop, listen, respond and choose to change. That is the beginning of transformation.

But there comes a time when learning is not enough. At that moment it's time to stop, listen, respond and choose to change. That is the beginning of transformation.

Scripture tells us that God has said we will not know the kingdom of heaven until we become like little children. Part of what I believe that means is that we must develop the qualities and skills many of us missed in childhood. Many of those qualities are connected to our feeling life. It was our wounded feelings that we learned to shut down. Those are the feelings we need to recapture and develop. When those feelings come alive, we will use them to recognize the clues and directions in our journey as the directions come from people, events and circumstances. However, we must emotionally sensitize ourselves to be able to pick up the clues.

This might be a good time to explain the difference between a *healthy* approach and an *unhealthy* approach to learning about the Child Within.

Healthy — To learn a childlike perspective and sensitivity. Feeling feelings . . . reclaiming lost childhood feelings, healing painful ones, celebrating happy ones.

Unhealthy — Childish, inappropriate behavior; sulking, controlling, pouting, carrying teddy bears to board meetings, acting fragile, avoiding personal responsibility, etc.

To develop the sensitivity of a child, one needs to risk recapturing emotional vulnerability.

1. First, we have to release the feelings that have been buried so very long and clear out the toxins of pain.
2. Next, we need to use childlike sensitivity to fill up our emotional life with the ability to experience new feelings of joy, pleasure, excitement, etc.

There is an old saying that feelings have two energy lives — once when they happen and once when discharged.

Healthy feeling life is when . . .
. . . . We feel a feeling
and
. . . . We express and discharge that feeling.

For many who have lived in relationships where expressing feelings were not taught or tolerated, there is a painful internal storehouse of feelings that need to be re-felt and then discharged. That's what recovery is all about. There is basically a three-point recovery plan.

_____●_____

For many who have lived in relationships where expressing feelings were not taught or tolerated, there is a painful internal storehouse of feelings that need to be re-felt and then discharged. That's what recovery is all about.

_____●_____

The Plan

1. Detox from the medicators that keep feelings under control and locked.

Medicating with outside substances
— Alcohol
— Drugs
— Nicotine
— Sugar

Medicating with behavior to release our own chemicals
— Frenetic activity
— Excessive sex
— Excessive spending
— Gambling
— Workaholism
— Binging/Purging

2. Discharge old stored feelings

Get good professional care (in-patient or out-patient treatment). Follow up with a support group.

This might be a good time to talk about the three kinds of support groups with positives and cautions.

	POSITIVES	CAUTIONS
12-Step Programs	1. Bonding 2. Spiritual journey 3. Healthy way of living is contained in the steps and traditions	1. Rigidity by members using 12-step programs. 2. Denial and resistance to treatment and therapy.
Leaderless Support Groups	1. Bonding 2. Identification 3. Sharing	1. Feelings and issues come up that no one has authority or training to address. Groups can become sessions of blame and anger.
Support Groups led by Qualified Professional	1. Bonding 2. Identification 3. Information 4. A safe place to share feelings and address issues	1. Be sure the therapist is well-qualified and knowledgeable about co-dependency. 2. Be aware of need to do your work and move on.

In my experience, some form of professional care, together with working a 12-step program, is a good recovery plan.

3. Fill up with the feelings of relief, happiness and joy.
Details later in the book.

By releasing the old painful feelings, we will be able to stop the compulsive and self-destructive behaviors we use to keep the pain and anxiety of these old feelings under control. What a gift we give ourselves when we decide we are too important to keep up the dependency/stuff-feelings/relief cycle!

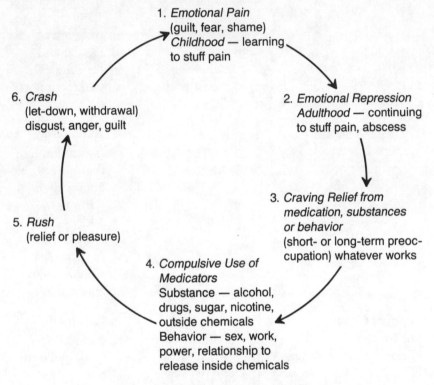

Figure 2. The Co-dependency Trap

As we medicate painful feelings, we can become drunk on our job, lover, partner, nicotine, sex, sugar, alcohol, excess exercise, etc. We can also become sober from each.

DRUNK means intoxicated, full of, overcome, muddled.

SOBER means moderate, nonindulgent, self-choosing, clear.

The way to recovery is feel/heal/change behavior. You cannot heal what you cannot feel, and you cannot feel what you medicate. First step first.

1. Stop medication (substance or behavior).

2. Feel the pain.
3. Heal the pain (re-feel and discharge).
4. Find emotional relief.
5. Make behavior changes.
6. Continue the healing.

Recovering from addictive disease and co-dependency is the jumping-off point for the continuation of the miracle.

Recovery is not for the faint-hearted, and there is no easy and simple way to do it. But the way is clear and the journey rewarding for those who choose to be spiritual warriors. Spiritual warriors are those who reclaim the souls of their Child Within and fill that child with spirit and feeling. In doing so, the child comes out of the darkness of pain and makes new choices to experience the light of recovery.

Spiritual warriors are those who reclaim the souls of their Child Within and fill that child with spirit and feeling.

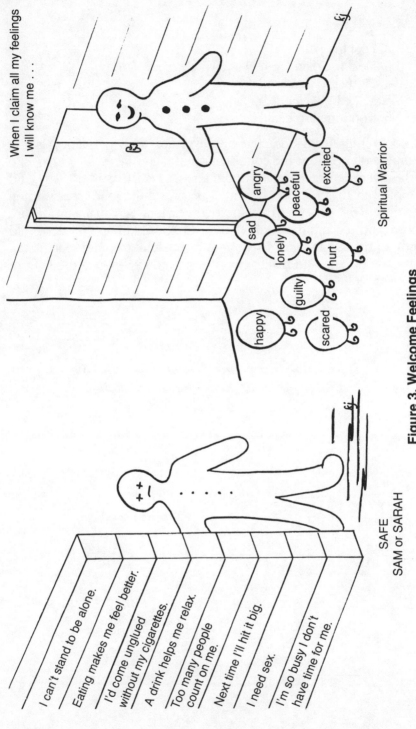

Figure 3. Welcome Feelings

6

Choose Risk And Change

When we get out of the dependency/relief cycle, we can start to make some new choices. It's hard to make choices when one is trapped in a cycle of compulsive behavior and action. The complaint of confusion often comes from those who do not make decisions to change behavior. Recovery and growth demand action and assertiveness. Sometimes it doesn't even matter if it's a good or bad decision. All that matters is that someone practices making a decision and does something different. One can learn from success or failure, so action (any action) is the positive step.

One can learn from success or failure, so action (any action) is the positive step.

The decision to "go to war" to care for oneself is necessary for full recovery.

19

Spiritual warriors have a few things in common:

1. **Spiritual warriors believe they have special gifts and a lifestyle to live.**
   They don't try to fit in or gain people's approval, and they don't respond to personal or professional "shoulds." They have learned to say no to others' demands and, most importantly, they have learned to say no to their own nagging self. Spiritual warriors accept themselves just the way they are.

2. **They are willing to invent new lifestyles.**
   Spiritual warriors recognize that during their time of co-dependent behavior they have surrounded themselves with people who are not helpful to their making changes in recovery. Sometimes these people are family members who are threatened by change, and sometimes they are fellow co-dependents who are also threatened by recovery changes. *The spiritual warrior learns that it is important to select a family of choice.* A family of choice is five to ten individuals who are in recovery and have good track records in making recovery decisions. They become role models and support-ive and confrontive friends during the time of recovery. For years recovering alcoholics have learned to "stick with the winners." Co-dependents need to learn the same lesson.

3. **They take risks.**
   A very important piece to a recovery lifestyle is to be able and willing to imagine and envision a lifestyle that is better than the one that feels painful. It is important to imagine and then take the necessary steps to make the vision come true. *Many risks will need to be taken.* One definition of the word "risk" is "investment." Taking risks is an investment in the kind of lifestyle you want for yourself. Freedom and happiness are not gifts. They are the by-product of the choices you make for yourself.

One of my favorite stories about risk-taking is my "Marty Mann" story. Marty Mann was a pioneering woman who was the founder of the National Council on Alcoholism. When she was at the peak of her success and I was a struggling newcomer to the field, trying to draw attention to the needs of families, she and I had a remarkable meeting.

I was speaking at a national conference for families sponsored by the National Council on Alcoholism. My presentation room was in the basement of a large hotel — hot, stuffy and crowded. No coffee or water. The rest of the conference sessions were in nice meeting rooms with air-conditioning and plenty of refreshments. As a recovering adult child of an alcoholic, I was just happy to be there — no matter how uncomfortable. I was still used to and willing to accept lesser treatment.

Halfway through my presentation, the audience revolted and demanded better treatment by the conference. I was swept along in the revolt, and about 300 people marched through the lobby of the hotel to a room paid for by a participant of the conference. We carried on with our conference in a private suite. About 20 minutes later, a knock on the door presented Marty Mann, honored guest of the conference. She asked for me by name. I was scared and afraid we had offended her.

She said to me, "Sharon, I'm thrilled. The spunk and integrity shown by this group of people is what I started the National Council on Alcoholism for. Keep the fires burning." With that, she was wheeled out in her wheelchair.

Some years later, after her death, I became the first woman to receive the Marty Mann award. The honor and thrill of the award was enriched by my memory of that encounter. Thank you, Marty.

4. **Spiritual warriors fail but learn from it.**
   Spiritual warriors have learned that actions teach the greatest lessons. For too long they have been data collectors. They have learned that too much information and too little action keeps one stuck and depressed. Spiritual warriors would rather make the wrong decision and learn a lesson than live in the illusion of safety, suffering greater unhappiness from the stuckness than from failure.

5. **Spiritual warriors trust their experiences.**
   There are memories of times of feeling wrong, bad, stupid and confused. Today spiritual warriors know that they can be still and listen to their own instincts and feelings. *They know there is a knowledge beyond information and that it has to*

do with recognizing feelings. Spiritual warriors have learned
to recognize and trust instinct and feelings.

6. **Spiritual warriors live in the present, not the past and not the future.**

   Two great robbers of serenity and recovery are the past and
   the future. *Both are nice places to visit through memory and
   vision, but a full life is lived in the present.* Spiritual warriors
   are so busy with current changes and happenings that they
   don't get bogged down with people and events they can't
   change.

7. **Spiritual warriors accept pain as necessary.**

   By studying the "lost and found" departments of their lives,
   they have learned that the lessons and rewards will come.
   Trust grows, they know their job is to feel all that happens.
   With the ability to feel feelings, spiritual warriors take the
   responsibility to feel, discharge and heal. Needing to
   understand and control becomes unimportant. Spiritual
   warriors do their part and know that the meaning will
   become clear over time.

8. **Spiritual warriors lead simple lives.**

   A wise mentor once said, "In all the confusions and conflicts
   of life, one lesson remains constant — simplify." It was easy
   when the choices were between bad and good. It became
   more difficult when the choices were between good and
   good. However, life is near fulfillment when the choices
   become between the best and the best.

   It's difficult to give up wonderful people, places and
   events, but it's often very necessary in order to have the time
   to experience and enjoy what we have. *In transformation,
   we learn to cut out excess baggage.* The simple will last. The
   way, the true way, needs little. When all our choices are
   between the best and the best, personal self-worth and
   recovery will be present.

*A wise mentor once said, "In all the
confusions and conflicts of life, one lesson
remains constant — simplify."*

9. **Spiritual warriors have developed the gift and skill of discernment.**

   There was a time when we were short on the supply of information about co-dependency and adult children. Today the supply is unlimited, and the wiser decisions are about discernment. *Discernment has to do with the choices to protect ourselves by setting boundaries around ourselves.* To allow ourselves to become content overloaded or experientially burned out is to abuse our well-being. It is important to read and attend experiences in direct proportion to being able to absorb and integrate what we take in. As adult children, we have shifted from "concerns with supply" to "concerns with selection." Recovery has very little to do with the continued understanding and redefining of the problem of co-dependency and adult children. As a matter of fact, the confusing over-abundance of new ways and new information to attempt to analyze and interpret the term co-dependency has become a source of confusion and familiar chaos to the co-dependent sufferer. Discernment is a welcome and important gift.

10. **Spiritual warriors accept recovery.**

    Sometimes there is nothing more to do than to enjoy recovery. Once we have reached that point, the only exciting and pleasurable next step is to share it. Someone once said, "It's good to be a seeker and a learner, but sooner or later, it's time to take what we have learned and begin to share with anyone who will listen."

"It's good to be a seeker and a learner,
but sooner or later, it's time to
take what we have learned and begin to
share with anyone who will listen."

There are two major stages in full recovery:

Stage 1: When we take what we need.

Stage 2: When we share what we have.

When we let go of the energy it takes to stay in pain we find the energy we need to get our needs met and to eventually help others get their needs met.

". . . . . . . Plant your own garden and decorate your own soul, instead of waiting for someone to send you flowers."

(From *Comes the Dawn,* Veronica Shoffstall)

7

Nurture Self

An important concept to remember is that life and recovery occur at the same time. The condition of "terminal seriousness" is one adult children and co-dependents have suffered from most of their lives. It's understandable. Oftentimes, there was very little to smile or laugh about. To learn to recognize humorous situations, to learn to laugh at oneself and to find the joy in little things is a great big part of recovery. It has been said that we have a "joy fitness;" some refer to laughter as "internal jogging." Norman Cousins tells us that laughter secretes endorphins that kill pain.

At a conference I heard Joel Goodman, a trainer with a sense of humor, list several workshop titles for helping professionals. These include:
- Creative suffering
- Overcoming peace of mind
- Guilt without sex
  etc., etc., etc.

He was able to coax a few smiles from his participants. He went on to say, "I try to take one day at a time, but sometimes several days happen to me at once." There were a few more giggles. Waking up the laughter response is necessary for full recovery.

Ashley Montagu says, *"Health is the ability to work, to love, to play and to use one's mind."* I would add that it is also necessary to be able to connect meaningfully with at least one other person and that health increases with the number of meaningful relationships.

There is good reason to "lighten up" when we realize that our major struggle is over.

1. We are here.
2. We have survived.
3. We deserve recovery.
4. We have choices to make it happen.

Many have not survived — many will never change. Psychiatrist and holocaust survivor Victor Frankl said, "The greatest need is to survive." Perhaps. However, I believe our greatest need is to belong. We all need to know that we matter to someone — friend, community, lover, mate, children.

The intimacy we all crave comes into our lives naturally when we become skilled at being an intimate. Becoming an intimate is our personal job and responsibility. One who has become an intimate is one who . . .

1. Is able to take care of his or her own personal, financial and emotional needs, and is not needy in any way.
2. Is alive with passion. Passion means full of life and feeling. Can appreciate sight, color, sound, touch and all the senses.
3. Has uncovered the long-lost feelings and has released, and forgiven when necessary, so they can come to a relationship emotionally clean and available.
4. Loves oneself enough to be clear enough to state wants and desires.
5. Has filled him or herself enough that they are now ready to give to another.

Two people who choose to share their intimacy skills with one another are able to connect fully and still let the winds of heaven dance between them.

Co-dependents tend to wait for the right person to come into their lives *or* for the person in their life to change. Recovering people *become* the right person, no matter what the cost or risk.

Let me repeat the steps to recognizing and partaking in the miracle:

1. Reframe thinking (Divine Protection).
2. Recognize Angels.
3. Understand "lost and found" areas of our life.
4. Welcome feelings.
5. Choose risk and change.
6. Nurture self.

Personal transformations are the day-to-day miracles we have all had and can learn to recognize and use more fully. To recognize that we have all survived many wounds starts the journey of recovery. But that's only the beginning. We are on the road to recovery and closer to our healing as we make the choices that bring about celebration. Each time we take another step and another risk, it's like coming out of a fog. We know it can get foggy again, but we've seen enough sunshine to know the fog won't last forever.

Each time we take another step and another risk, it's like coming out of a fog. We know it can get foggy again, but we've seen enough sunshine to know the fog won't last forever.

The sunshine and light of the spirit frees people. It gives them power and strength and fosters transformation. Transforming people are choicemakers. I call them *Springtime People*. No matter what the season, they . . .

1. Radiate new life and hope.
2. Make necessary choices.
3. Celebrate life with laughter and joy.

Each is like the note of a song, and when they get together, the music they make has harmony and joy.

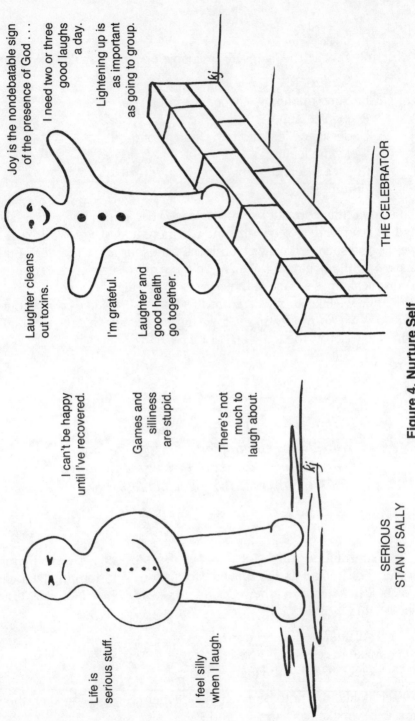

Figure 4. Nurture Self

Part Two

Understanding
Co-dependency

Understanding Co-dependency

Many find their recognition of "the Miracle" when they recover from addictive disease — many when they learn about co-dependency.

The Confusion

The good news is that so many people now have options to recover from addictive disease, co-dependency and the issues that occur as a result of coming from a dysfunctional family. The bad news is that there seem to be so many approaches, different frameworks and overwhelming information that sometimes it is difficult to get a clear understanding of the disease and formulate a clear recovery plan.

To begin, let's look at what co-dependency is. It is possible to identify with the disease and yet get trapped in an overwhelming glut of books, tapes, groups, therapists, frameworks and approaches that leave you feeling overwhelmed and more defeated than you felt before you ever heard the word "co-dependency."

Some of the old phrases that many people heard around early 12-step recovery were, "Keep it simple," "Stick with the winners" and "Be good to yourself." These are just as true today in looking at the disease of co-dependency as they have always been in the disease of chemical addiction. It is my hope that this book will clarify, simplify and offer you some hope and encouragement in your own recovery process.

In the last few years many of us have been trying to understand what co-dependency is all about. In many ways, it's like being at a smorgasbord of information. You know that no matter how good it all is, you still get a stomachache and a bloated feeling if you eat too much too fast. It's a real challenge to pick out two or three of your

favorite items, enjoy them fully and at another date maybe pick two
or three more.

Recovery is so much easier to grasp if we take it in small, manageable pieces and heal in small ways, rather than trying to do it all at
once and wearing ourselves out with too much too soon. Without
timing, learning about and recovering from this disease can be
another form of self-abuse. And yet with so much available, we would
be foolish not to begin our recovery program.

The word "discernment" means "having the ability to separate, to
perceive, to be clear and to make good judgments." Discernment is
needed now in learning which framework to use or direction to take,
which part of the disease to work on first, or which kind of group to
attend.

. . . . Many people will come into one of our programs and say,

> "Hi, my name is so-and-so, and I'm a recovering alcoholic, a
> recovering drug addict, a current nicotine addict, a recovering sex
> addict, a current overeater, but I just don't know where to begin. When
> I recovered from my chemical addiction, I really thought I had it
> made, and yet there were many things that were still troubling me,
> such as my relationship with my spouse. Today I just feel that I've got
> so many things wrong with me, I don't know where to begin or what
> to do first and some days I wonder if I can even hang on to my
> sobriety and ability to stay clean. Can you help?"

. . . . Or we'll hear someone else come in and say,

> "I first approached help because I was interested in a meaningful
> relationship, and now I'm going to five different kinds of meetings six
> nights a week, plus trying to hold down my job. I don't have time to
> build a relationship now even if I did meet the one I'd like to be
> with."

. . . . Another will say,

> "I'm working so hard on my program that I have new problems
> occurring with my relationship with my children, and I'm probably
> going to have to work on that sometime. It seems that by the time I
> do everything I'm supposed to do in my aftercare plan, there is not
> enough time for the people in my life. Some days I just wonder if any
> of it is worth it."

It is clear to me that we are drowning in knowledge and information and still starved for healing and direction.

―――――――――――――――●―――――――――――――――

It is clear to me that we are drowning in knowledge and information and still starved for healing and direction.

―――――――――――――――●―――――――――――――――

8

What Is
Co-dependency?

Co-dependency has a set of symptoms, a course of progression and complications if it is not interrupted and treated. So often the word has been used in such loose ways that it has lost its meaning. Some even mistake ordinary acts of kindness or deep caring and love as co-dependency. Others generalize, making it a cultural condition affecting everyone.

Co-dependency is a disease. It is a specific condition characterized by preoccupation and extreme dependency on another person (emotionally, socially, sometimes physically) or on a substance (such as alcohol, drugs, nicotine and sugar) or on a behavior (such as workaholism, gambling, compulsive sexual acting out). This dependence, nurtured over a long period of time, becomes a pathological condition that affects the co-dependent in all other relationships.

It seems that a popular theme emerges as another core issue every few months. It's cultural dependency, crystal power, root shame, pre-memory sexual abuse, etc. To keep up with each new approach almost demands that getting therapy becomes a lifestyle instead of an enhancement to living. It is no wonder that serenity, inner peace and satisfying relationships are so hard to attain and maintain.

---

*To keep up with each new approach almost
demands that getting therapy becomes
a lifestyle instead of an enhancement
to living.*

Recovery isn't about doing. It's about "being" — being fully alive, aware and invested in day-to-day reality, meaning and joy. To develop a dependency on recovering is just to switch to another dependency. Therapy is important and it has its place. Therapy is a healing of wounded minds, emotions and spirits, just the way physical therapy, such as surgery, is necessary for a wounded body.

We have learned to visit a doctor when our body needs care, to let the body heal and then to get on with life. The same opportunity is there for our feelings and spirit if we learn to use the healing processes and then to get on with life.

To build a framework for simplifying recovery, let's begin by learning just what co-dependency is.

Co-dependency is "a system of inhuman rules and expectations that are passed down from generation to generation," says Robert Subby in *Lost In The Shuffle: The Co-dependent Reality*. It is an enmeshment of toxic relationships.

My own definition of co-dependency is that it is a toxic relationship to a substance, a person or a behavior that leads to self-delusion, emotional repression and compulsive behavior that results in increased shame, low self-worth, relationship problems and medical complications.

My own definition of co-dependency is that it is a toxic relationship to a substance, a person or a behavior that leads to self-delusion, emotional repression and compulsive behavior that results in increased shame, low self-worth, relationship problems and medical complications.

Distorted thinking or self-delusion comes from not having a full awareness of our reality. It's having a limited view of reality.

Each member of a family has a view of what's going on that is different from every other member's. Families are opportunities for dialogue and sharing. In healthy families people do share and each person gets a bigger view. In unhealthy families people hear and respect only their own view. They are sure that their view is the right view and their perspective is the right perspective.

9

Symptoms

Symptom 1: Delusion (Distorted Thinking)

Delusion is when we allow our thoughts to get distorted by not taking in all the information that is there. Instead we live with our own narrow view of what we see and how we see it.

In unhealthy families people are taught either directly or indirectly not to be honest with all they see, hear and feel. And what they begin to learn in a painful family is how to separate themselves from that total view and live with a limited view.

Many of us, in different ways, have disassociated from "how it was" and chosen to believe "how we want it to be." *When we disassociate from the reality of what we truly feel, we are being dishonest with ourselves.* So distorted thinking is lying to yourself and to others about the pain you're in. It is not experiencing the whole picture.

Symptom 2: Emotional Repression (Distorted Feeling)

Each time we disassociate from reality and deny what is happening, we repress or stuff the feelings that go with the event. Shutting down those feelings becomes a condition of emotional repression. After a while as time goes by, the feelings that one shuts down and refuses to feel become all mixed together. This emotional mixture is called *undifferentiated emotion.* That means we don't even know what we feel anymore. Is it anger, guilt, hurt, shame? What is it? The events get lost. First of all, we are denying the events. And over time the events get lost and people experience free-floating feelings (free-floating anxiety).

This is undifferentiated emotion that churns inside, giving us emotional pain.

Now it's important that we know about what churns inside — because it is this pain that causes our craving for relief. We crave some kind of relief from what we feel.

Symptom 3: Compulsive Behavior (Distorted Behavior)

Over the years for children from painful homes, there has been an inner cesspool or emotional abscess of shame, hurt, loneliness, anger, inadequacy, sadness and hopelessness. It is deep inside and kept locked away. It hurts, and the need for relief from the pain becomes a craving.

The first stage of dependency is to seek some sort of change of mood that is pleasurable or relief-producing.

Different substances and behaviors work for different people. Some find one of the predictable mood-changing substances such as alcohol. If the person is set up genetically to react to mood-changing chemicals, dependency and addiction begin.

The chemicals provide relief from that deeply buried inner pain. It is a temporary relief, but for those whose bodies react addictively, it is a potent one which works every time. Drugs and alcohol are effective pain relievers. So is nicotine.

Smoking interferes with the attainment of intimacy and personal growth. Smoking serves as a security blanket — or an insulator from the world of uncertainty and psychic pain.

By turning to cigarettes during times of stress, people are less likely to find strength within themselves. In a sense for many people, tobacco is being held onto as that one last crutch.

———————————————•———————————————

*Smoking interferes with the attainment of
intimacy and personal growth. Smoking serves
as a security blanket — or an insulator from
the world of uncertainty and psychic pain.*

———————————————•———————————————

Crutches are interesting things. When a leg is broken, it's just the
thing to help you get around. But after the leg has mended, it is vital
that the crutch be put back into the closet. Otherwise the leg's
muscle will shrivel from disuse and eventually become so weak and
withered as to become truly useless — and chronically in need of
a crutch.

So many people, smokers and nonsmokers alike, have withered
emotional muscles. For whatever reasons at some point in our lives
we decided to lean upon a drink, some other drug, a cigarette, an
unhealthy relationship or something else in order to help deal with
emotional discomfort. And it worked for a while. Unfortunately, long
after the precipitating events which made smoking or whatever seem
so attractive had passed, the crutch remained. And remained and
remained. Meanwhile, the emotional muscle deteriorated beyond its
original fragile condition — further increasing dependence upon
the crutch.

There are a variety of crutches and reliefs. Some rushes and some
reliefs last 20 minutes, some last 10, some last up to an hour, but as
you use them you begin to program yourself to get some kind of
relief from that anxiety you feel.

Not everybody is set up to be able to get that kind of relief from
alcohol and drugs. It just doesn't work for them because they do not
have the genetic make-up for it. It doesn't work for everybody. So
there are many more people who have lived in painful homes who
need relief and who have this craving than can successfully use drugs
and alcohol.

These people find other things, depending on their circumstances,
depending on their family system, depending on what works for
them. Some people are set up to be sugar-sensitive, and for them,

sugar does what alcohol does not do. For families that are very perfectionistic, stoic and cognitive, people are set up to get a rush through the power of control. Some find their rush through self-control or controlling others, and others need to control circumstances and events. In those kinds of families, we find the anorexic — the person who starves and gets a rush from being able to turn away food. Some get good feelings from compulsive overeating. There is a reward with food consumption.

Eating disorders are a chronic, progressive and sometimes fatal disease if left untreated. This disease affects the physical, psychological, social and spiritual areas of a person's life and requires a lifelong program of recovery.

Eating disorders are a chronic, progressive and sometimes fatal disease if left untreated.

Symptoms of eating disorders include the following:

- Preoccupation with food and weight
- Social isolation as a result of food use
- Use of food to change or moderate feelings
- Repeated and unsuccessful attempts to diet
- Compulsive exercising or not exercising at all
- Fasting
- Self-induced vomiting
- Frequent overeating — binge-eating
- Laxative and/or diuretic abuse
- Self anger due to food abuse
- Low self-esteem

Anorexia nervosa is a relentless pursuit of thinness, characterized by self-starvation, compulsive exercise and laxative abuse. *Bulimia* is the addictive binge/purge cycle characterized by compulsively eating, then purging by self-induced vomiting or laxative abuse.

In cognitive, perfectionistic families we also find the workaholic rush. These people stay at a certain tolerable level of their internal pain by staying frenetically active. They are always busy accomplishing, doing one more thing, achieving one more goal. They go from one thing to another, accomplishing great things . . . or nothing.

---

*In cognitive, perfectionistic families we also
find the workaholic rush. These people
stay at a certain tolerable level of their internal
pain by staying frenetically active.*

People can get their rush in a variety of ways. People can rush with what we call "green-paper" addiction. That's the whole realm of how people spend money. It ranges all the way from occasional overspending to living on credit cards, never really believing you have to pay them off. Green-paper addiction includes gambling, which is one of the toughest of the compulsions to treat. The seduction of gambling is a powerful dependency issue.

Drugs, alcohol, nicotine and sugar are the most common chemical substances with which people form toxic relationships. Many of the other toxicities are in behaviors . . . bulimia, anorexia, some compulsive eating, gambling, workaholism and relationship dependency.

Sexuality

I'd like to talk more specifically about sexuality because in treating co-dependency, we also see many sexual problems and dysfunctions.

There are many different ways to look at what happens to people struggling with sexual behavioral problems and sexual dysfunctions. I view sexual acting out as a co-dependency compulsion that is treatable.

We become very dependent on and even skilled with the seduction aspect of a relationship. This is because seduction is very emotional. You share feelings, you have this stirring inside, this sharing of information and vulnerability. For the adult child or the co-dependent who suffers from lack of feelings available to them, seduction is exciting and pleasure-producing.

It is enticing to become trapped in a cycle of seduction, getting a rush from the romantic beginnings of a new sexual relationship or from a new conquest. But when the excitement of the seduction phase of a relationship ends, *they are unable to access their deeper feelings and move on to a genuinely passionate relationship.* If you look it up in a dictionary, the word "passion" means "full of feeling." When we get ready to have a close relationship, we can see that we are dependent on our own ability to be full of feeling before we can experience intimacy.

When we get ready to have a close relationship, we can see that we are dependent on our own ability to be full of feeling before we can experience intimacy.

Intimacy is the coming together of feelings and may or may not include sexual contact. A term that I use in describing that coming together is "emotional intercourse."

A passionless relationship is what too many adult children and co-dependents have settled for because their feelings have been medicated. Passion has to do with waking up one's own life and becoming a passionate person.

People who have chosen to do that become capable of intimacy and full emotional intercourse. They can then have a very potent physical intercourse as well.

Co-dependency treatment and the waking up of those feelings help one become able to act from a passion base. It is probable that treatment will eliminate the sexual compulsions for those who are willing to take the recovery route.

Whether the compulsion is . . .
  Overeating
  Refusing food
  Acting out sexually
  Workaholism
  Power
  Nicotine (Physical addiction)
  Alcohol (Physical addiction)
  Drugs (Physical addiction)
  Sugar (Physical addiction)

The symptoms of the disease are simply . . .
  . . . . . Denial (Toxic thinking)
  . . . . . Emotional repression (Toxic stuffing of feelings)
  . . . . . Compulsion (Toxic behaving)

If these symptoms go unchecked, they develop complications.

10

Complications

Complication 1: Low Self-Worth (Shame)

The first complication of co-dependency is chronic low self-worth (a condition of feeling shame). This shame is not the same as guilt.

1. Guilt is felt when one does something to harm oneself or others. "I feel badly about something." The wonderful thing about guilt, and the reason guilt can be such a positive feeling, is that when I recognize it, I can make amends and then feel good about myself. Guilt has a pattern that brings us back to our good feeling if we pursue it. Every piece of guilt can be amended one way or another. So guilt is a productive feeling. To feel guilty in places where it's appropriate and then begin to make amends is to be on a straight path to self-worth and healing.

Guilt is the feeling: "I've done something bad and I would like to make amends about it and change." Shame is different.

45

---

*Guilt is a productive feeling. To feel
guilty in places where it's appropriate
and then begin to make amends is to be on
a straight path to self-worth and healing.*

---

2. Shame is feeling that "I am what is bad." I am bad — not that
I did something bad, I just am faulty. I'm damaged goods. I am bad.
Dysfunctional families tend to produce shame-based people. In
hurting families people bring generations of shame into their current
life. What does not get resolved in the generation before comes as a
package. It's part of the shame. The shame about . . .

Alcoholism	Sexual abuse
Suicide	Drug addiction
Bulimia	Affairs
Overweight	Workaholism
Anorexia	Gambling
Poverty	Wealth

It's what came with my package and I feel ashamed about that.

Then when you add all those old family rules, those inhuman
rules, what you end up with is people who feel "less
than" . . . "unworthy." They end up with what I call *chronic low self-
worth,* which is being *shame-based.* They are the same thing. When
we are shame-based, then it is very difficult to make decisions on
behalf of what we need for ourselves. People get into this place of
perceived powerlessness. They believe that they are bad and
unworthy and there is nothing they can do to change. People stay in
painful circumstances, jobs and relationships because they feel they
do not deserve anything any better.

Complication 2: Relationship Problems

The co-dependent lives with environmental wars. The smallest
unit is the couple. It is rare to find relationship satisfaction when one
is emotionally frozen and behaviorally compulsive. Knowing and

responding to a partner is simply not the major focus. Beyond the coupling, the family, friends, the job and work environment all suffer from lack of focus and commitment.

Learning to clearly face the reality of hurting relationships is the first step of recovery. Next comes the behavioral rebuilding of relationships one values. There may be family-of-origin relationships (mother, father, siblings). It may include current relationships (mate, lover, children, friends, etc.). Some toxic relationships need to end, and others need to be rebuilt. All relationships deserve attention in co-dependency recovery.

Complication 3: Medical Complications

There's one more complication. If through low self-worth and shame we do not make changes, we will stay stuck. *Stuckness is another word for a subtle death wish.* People who are stuck are beginning the dying process. But earlier in this stuckness we start having medical problems. When we do not reach out and ask for what we need and get ourselves nourished, our bodies get out of harmony, out of alignment, out of ease and they become diseased. We "make ourselves sick."

When we are functioning in harmony and perceive ourselves as high functioning, we'll stay healthier. When we perceive ourselves as low-energy, stuck, down, powerless, we become more susceptible to illness.

Young children often suffer from asthma, allergies and chronic colds and flu. Older people suffering from co-dependency report migraines, colitis, intestinal problems and other stress-related illnesses. In our work we have seen a frequent incidence of cancer in co-dependents.

Two good books to read to understand further the relationship between our emotions and cancer are *Getting Well Again* by Carl Simington and *Love, Medicine and Miracles* by Bernie Siegel.

11

Treatment
And Recovery

The good news is that co-dependency is treatable with appropriate approaches.

Effective Treatment

1. Confronts self-delusion with new information. With learning comes understanding.
2. Creates a safe atmosphere where feelings can surface to be shared and discharged so healing can take place.
3. Provides an atmosphere where it is safe and possible to detach from compulsive behavior.

The miracle of recovery is there for those who choose to make new choices and decisions.

Recovery needs a program of therapy PLUS a 12-step support system.

The co-dependent does best with a two-part recovery program. One part is involvement in a 12-step group, and the other part is a relationship with a co-dependency therapist or a professionally led group.

---

*The miracle of recovery is there for those who
choose to make new choices and decisions.*

So often we see a co-dependent who is going to three or four different kinds of 12-step programs, perhaps a leaderless ACoA group and not getting any professional therapy. People in this kind of situation are often confused, angry and overwhelmed. Even though they are going to many meetings, they still do not feel focused, resolved or in recovery. As the co-dependent uncovers more and more memories, begins to feel more and more feelings, and their life situations become more complex, it is important for this person to get professional care. They need this help to make necessary decisions, to receive guidance while walking through the journey of uncovering feelings and to have some input and reality checked through someone qualified to give it.

I tell co-dependents that it is not necessary to go to many different types of 12-step programs. The focus of 12-step work is to work the steps. They work the same way whether one is concerned with compulsive eating, compulsive gambling, compulsive acting out sexually, etc. The compulsion that one exhibits is the doorway to a program of recovery. One can be working any compulsion with the 12 steps and not need to go to a separate group for each issue.

---

*The compulsion that one exhibits is the doorway
to a program of recovery. One can be working
any compulsion with the 12 steps and not
need to go to a separate group for each issue.*

Therefore, I recommend that people pick one or two 12-step programs to attend that fit with the major compulsion that they are struggling with. They should also reserve time and energy to invest in a therapeutic process, choosing a therapist to work with in co-dependency recovery who thoroughly understands the disease concept of co-dependency. If that person has come from a painful family of their own, it is crucial that they have already received and healed in their own treatment process.

Therapy can come in many forms. It can be an outpatient program. It can be a short, intense program, of eight to ten days. What is important is that the program be specifically designed and facilitated by people who are specifically trained in co-dependency work. Therapy can and does come to an end.

Therapy can and does come to an end.

Continued involvement in a 12-step program can be a much longer commitment. The analogy I sometimes use is that a good treatment program is like emotional surgery. It is a place to do a lot of work all at once. Emotional surgery is then followed by long-term healing, which takes place in 12-step support groups.

I sometimes see recovery as a beautiful big mansion with all kinds of possibilities and rooms and explorations and new styles and new horizons. The mansion is there for anyone who wants to walk through the door. And there are many doors to this mansion. One can come in through the door of alcoholism, the door of sexual compulsion, the door of eating disorders, the door of workaholism, the door of nicotinism, the door of relationship dependency.

Each one of these doors is an entry point that one can recognize in oneself. But once you walk through the door, the differences are diminished and similarities emphasized.

---

*But once you walk through the door, the
differences are diminished and
the similarities emphasized.*

Once through the door, the disease of co-dependency has to do with a personal struggle with a variety of compulsive behaviors. All the people walking through the door have lived in a condition of low self-worth, feeling deep shame, inadequacy and anger. All the people inside the mansion are exploring the same recovery, the search for a healing of self. Once through the door, we are all much more alike than different and the focus on recovery can be supportive, simple and clear.

In summary, regardless of the compulsion one experiences, the way to healing and recovery is quite similar. We need to reverse the process of the disease. We need to move from disease to recovery and healing.

DISEASE (Symptoms)	RECOVERY AND HEALING
1. Self-delusion	To admit our lives are unmanageable and we need help.
2. Emotional repression	Stop medicating feelings with substances and behaviors and allow ourselves to reconnect with our feeling life.
3. Compulsive behavior	Become abstinent from toxic substances and change behavior in toxic relationships.

DISEASE (Complications)	RECOVERY AND HEALING
1. Chronic low self-worth	Take the risks and make the changes to care for oneself.
2. Relationship problems	Change behaviors to rebuild valued relationships and end or change toxic ones.
3. Medical complications	Seek appropriate help.

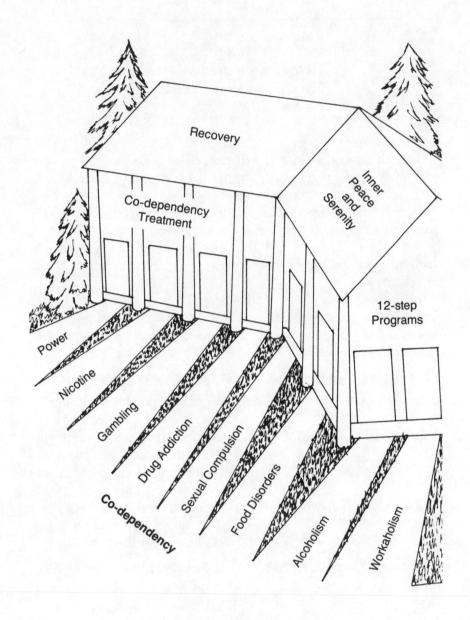

Figure 5. Recovery Mansion

There is a need for a plan for recovery.

1. Join one or at maximum, two, 12-step support groups to address one or two primary compulsions. Fit all other compulsions into these two meetings. There is simply no need to attend five or six different 12-step programs or to go to a meeting every night for a long period of time. The promise of inner peace, reconciliation and healing is there for those who choose to *work* a recovery program of risk, choice and change. Too often, recovery is a series of revolving doors.

2. Seek treatment (in- or out-patient) with someone specifically trained in co-dependency treatment. Plan a one- or two-year program. Treat your recovery as you would any other medical recovery. It needs the stages of intensive care, aftercare and lifestyle change.

12

False Enlightenment

There are many who would like to feel inner peace and the serenity of healing before going through the pain of releasing the inner abscess. It is possible to block and deny our pain, but eventually through rigidity or physical illness, it catches up with us. It is good to beware of easy fixes. We need to be cautious about methods that suggest we band-aid our years of frozen or repressed pain and cover it up with "enlightenment," rather than the unfolding of true inner and outer "enlightenment" that comes with healing.

The point of recovering and finding your spirituality is to enhance healing and self-love, not to further punish yourself or hide in unreality. There are no short-cuts. It is necessary to go through each stage of re-feeling, healing and recovery. Be sure to take the healing route, instead of the escape route. In short, it is healthy to DESCEND before you TRANSCEND.

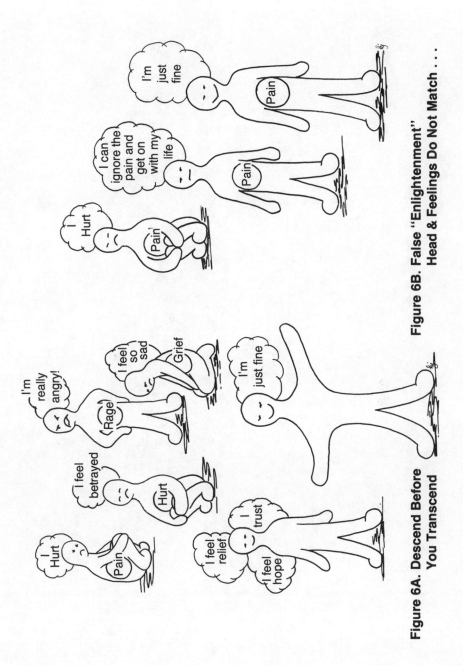

Figure 6B. False "Enlightenment"
Head & Feelings Do Not Match . . .

Figure 6A. Descend Before
You Transcend

Part Three
Growing-Up Years

13

My Early Years

It has been helpful for me to see my childhood and growing-up years as an observer. It has helped me to feel safe as an adult observing a childhood experience. I needed a sense of understanding before I allowed myself to feel it all. I needed a lot of information to help me, and yet I would have resisted getting it if I had known how much I was going to hurt.

I was born into a family of love and pain. My mother was a lost soul in the family that she grew up in. Her dad had come from the Old Country and tried to make good in a small Minnesota farming community. Her mom was a small town, local girl. There were struggles. Her father was a Protestant, controlling and rigid. He won the love of the community's prettiest girl, 15 years younger than he was. His young and beautiful wife was a handful, full of spunk and spirit. She was also a Catholic. They married, much to the dismay of all concerned. In the years that followed, including the Depression, my grandpa failed with his plans and his work efforts. Grandma carried on having babies and providing a living for the family by working outside the home. Strong female leadership was always a part of my history.

Grandma's first child was a son. He was the number one special child from the day he was born until the day he died. Their second child was a daughter. This daughter was clearly in the shadow of her brother and withdrew shyly as a lesser person in the family. She was my mother. Sad and lonely, withdrawn as a youngster, she was followed by a beautiful young sister who was special and a baby sister who was often sick. My mother was truly a lost child.

There was love in this family. It was a musical, affectionate and loving group. I remember many fun events. Sunday afternoons were often spent playing the piano and singing, with lots of good food, meals eaten together and affectionate hugs and laughter. The contrast between warmth and loss, happiness and hurt was both attracting and crazy-making.

Grandpa sought relief and comfort in wine and swallowed his losses quietly, being in the hospital on and off for many ailments. Grandpa's addiction was never identified as such, even though I learned much later on that he dried out from time to time in hospitals. Grandma was strong, loving and caretaking.

My father's family was also very painful. His father was a potato baron in southern Minnesota, and was also a bootlegger in the early days. First he made "potato liquor," then he learned new and better ways to make liquor. He used what he made to make more, and needed a large family to help him in the potato fields.

Anger, drunkenness and physical abuse were regular occurrences in my father's family. When he was only seven, his mother could no longer cope. She ran away. She left five children old enough to care for themselves and survive. She also left an eleven-year-old and a seven-year-old, my father. He lived with his abusive and drunk father for two years. Then his father died. He was now nine and alone. A family took him in and he worked to pay for his food and lodging. School was not an option. My father was also a lost child.

When my mother was a teen and my father all of twenty, they began to date. Mother was mesmerized by this brash, bold, exciting boy who found and sought her. My father was thrilled to have someone specifically interested in him. *Two lost souls found each other before they ever found themselves.* From the things that they told me, from letters I have that they wrote to each other, from comments from relatives, I have learned of a beautiful, yet desperate love story.

My father drank a lot. In those early days when life was still manageable, they seemed to have a wonderful time. The relationship between my mom and dad was built on shaky underpinnings of loss and grief, fear and inadequacy. Yet with love, laughter and the medication of alcohol, it seemed to all that there was a lot of joy, excitement and hope.

It was into this paradox that I was born. My earliest memories are of *outside* family fun and laughter and togetherness, and *inside* fears and feelings that I couldn't name or understand. I only knew that in the midst of what looked okay to me, my stomach would get very sick or my heart would pound. Today I have names for those feelings that I didn't have then. My growing-up years were a continuation of learning to live a double life. It had pain on the inside, normal happenings and happiness on the outside.

With two lost children as parents, I became the family hero or the special focus as a very young child. I received lots of love and attention. By the third grade, I was aware that I was special to my mom and dad and my grandma and grandpa and to my aunt Gertie. Because of this specialness, I also felt responsible for them. Each in their own way had let me know what they needed from me. And I learned very early that my role was to make others happy and fulfill their needs. This early learning stayed with me for many years until the first major awareness in my life.

My father was an alcoholic. It took a long time for me to be able to admit that my father drank, that his drinking was not only self-destructive, but also nearly destroyed my family. It took many years for me to understand that my father suffered from the disease of alcoholism.

During his lifetime no one in our family would have called him an alcoholic. I grew up in a small town, a rural community, population 600, where the term "alcoholic" was never used. We used euphemisms and synonyms, but we never labeled a heavy drinker an "alcoholic."

Instead, we said: "He drinks too much." And a person who drank too much . . .

— really got loaded
— was flying high
— was schnookered, blasted, looped, tipsy.

Of course, it was easy to see that the drinker was "feeling good, feeling no pain."

There were winos, town drunks and bums. But we never called anyone an alcoholic.

My Family

At times my family was a joy. I thought I could never be happier. We had picnics, parties, much food and good times. But we also had bad times, times of anger and bitterness, times of fear and confusion. Like most people, I experienced moodiness and periods of intense loneliness.

When a friend would ask me about my family, I would eagerly talk about the joy, the pleasantries. And I would keep the bad parts, the miserable experiences, hidden inside. I could not reconcile the good times with the bad times. I couldn't understand the inconsistencies in my family, the wild swings from happiness to despair.

Consequently, I felt confused . . . deeply confused.

The Good Times

Living in a small town meant that my family knew almost everyone in town. Everyone knew us. I grew up surrounded by people and activity — never a dull moment. To me, the drugstore was a bazaar of fascinating trinkets, baubles and exotic perfumes and colognes. It was the only place in town you could get a genuine cherry phosphate soda, a drink that sparkled on your tongue and tickled your nose. And the drugstore had a comic book bin where you could browse for hours over the latest amazing exploits of Superman and Wonderwoman and Submarine Man, and of course, Batman and Robin. There was also a general clothing store that contained a fashion shop devoted to all the mysterious paraphernalia of womanhood.

The town boasted a movie theater where we noisily reveled in the Saturday afternoon matinees. At intermissions we converged on the mechanical marvel . . . a popcorn machine . . . on wheels.

There was a post office with "Wanted" pictures of fugitives and desperadoes posted on the wall. There was a telephone switchboard with an operator who placed the calls, a hospital, gas stations and a community hall.

My father owned a major business in town, and our family was respected by the community. We fit in. We belonged. I was proud of our little town, and I sensed that other people in our community were proud of my family and proud of me.

I was a first child and also a first grandchild. I have felt special since I was a little girl. My father told me over and over, "Sharon, you are special, very special, and you can do anything."

My aunts and uncles liked having me visit. And my relatives took an interest in my schoolwork and extracurricular activities. Time and again they came to watch me act in school plays. And when I debated or participated in oratory and public-speaking contests, my relatives were a supportive and sympathetic audience. I felt that they took a real interest in me, that they cared about what I did. I felt I could rely on them.

I spent a lot of time with my grandma in my early years. I was her first grandchild. She taught me about the warmth and love of God, and I grew up with a deep faith and trust in a higher power.

My family and friends liked to have a good time — they liked games, special occasions, parties. My dad played softball and in the summer the whole family would go to the games to watch him play. Of course, there was always lots of cold beer at the ballgames and after the games, but as all the players said, "It wouldn't be a ballgame without beer."

We also had an annual Fourth of July family shindig, a big family party. We'd go to a nearby state where fireworks were legal and buy several hundred dollars' worth of firecrackers, cherry bombs, sparklers and rockets. Then we'd set up a fireworks display at my uncle's farm. The whole town would come for a spectacular evening of slightly illegal pyrotechnics. There was always drinking, but the drinking was part of the social occasion.

We spent hours around the piano singing. It was our home entertainment center. Grandma played by ear, and I read music. Each Sunday afternoon we had a sing-along. We laughed and joked and sang old familiar melodies and some of the newer tunes. My father's favorite was *You Always Hurt the One You Love*. I still have the sheet music.

Sundays also meant Sunday dinner with chicken or roast beef, potatoes and gravy, homemade rolls . . . and always a couple of extra places set at the table for friends, for company. My mother was a fantastic cook, and my mouth still waters at memories of Christmas candy, mashed potatoes and old-fashioned gravy and homemade cinnamon rolls.

During family get-togethers my dad played host, seeing to it that everyone had plenty to eat and plenty to drink. He'd see to it that plates were heaped, glasses well-filled.

"Have some more," he'd urge. "Better have another helping of those peas and carrots."

After dinner there was dessert — homemade pie or cake or cobbler. He heaped generous portions on every plate. Dad grew up in a family of want and need, and he wanted to share his prosperity.

My early years were quite happy. With my family, I especially remember being touched with affection, respect and love. I remember a soul-warming sense of comfort.

Yet even at this time, even when I felt happy and content, I also felt at times an underlying sense of uneasiness. I didn't know why.

I didn't tell anyone. It was as if I wore a veneer of serenity — all smiles and charm and conviviality. But inside my heart would pound furiously and I would tremble with fear. I didn't know why.

Sometimes my parents did things I couldn't understand. Very quickly my dad could be irritable over small things — a tear in the screen door, a scratch on the car fender. He seemed pressured and he'd get madder and madder. Enraged, he'd yell at my mom, me or my brother. Dad would start blaming, as if it were important to establish once and for all who was responsible for every problem. This started when I was about 12 years old. I felt like I'd been bad, unspeakably bad — like I'd done something terrible and disgraced my father. I never understood the reasons for this angry behavior.

When we had company, when friends or neighbors visited, my family seemed to be together, seemed to be amiable and cordial and happy together. But when friends left, the facade lifted, the amiability and happiness vanished, and it was replaced by tension and anger and tears. My mother cried a lot. And I felt trapped in strange, uncomfortable emotions. But I couldn't tell anyone, not even my closest friends.

When I was five years old, I ran away from home again and again. I remember being found in a neighbor's attic. Another time my parents found me hiding out in the cemetery. I recall wandering alone down the aisles of a train. But they always found me. They always brought me back.

I ran and ran, but I don't remember what I was running away from.

I also recall the discomfort and nausea of car-sickness whenever I left home, especially if for one dimly comprehended reason or another, I was being sent away to stay with relatives.

Running. Escape. Inside I wanted to run and yet I didn't want to leave. I felt alone, empty, sick. I wanted someone to hold me, to listen to my innermost fears and conflicts.

And yet when I was around those I loved most, I felt physically ill. Desolate and uncomprehending, I prayed for help.

Tired and defeated, I started to miss school. I played "sick" about once a week in my early school years. Grandma would then make a fuss over me and I'd get lots of love and attention. The nights were the worst times. I could hear my mother and father arguing. ". . . money . . ." ". . . too expensive . . ." ". . . bills . . ."

There was a lot of tension about finances. But there was an even stronger undercurrent of bad feelings that came out when they argued about their relationship, the lack of closeness my mother felt, and her yearning for more time together. My dad would end up yelling. My mom would cry. And I would cover my head and pretend not to hear. But I couldn't avoid the noisy confrontations. I shuddered when the clamor started, and my stomach knotted up and ached.

I used to make up my own world, a place where it was pretty, quiet and safe. It felt good to lose myself in reverie, to have a fantasy world of my own making, where no one ever worried or argued or cried.

The Elementary School Years

In grade school I found a way to escape. I worked hard. I did everything my teachers asked. They liked me and praised my compliance, my eager and industrious attitude toward schoolwork. I learned to read early, and I did my assignments promptly. I wasn't a dawdler. I was always good with words and I was religious.

In Catholic grade school I had nuns as teachers. Sister Beatrice paid special attention to me when I felt down, when I was troubled by my homelife but couldn't talk about it. She'd tell me, "Sharon, you have a great talent and determination. You'll manage in this life — you'll manage and survive."

Sister Beatrice told me this and I believed her. I flourished in school. The teachers' praise felt good. I worked hard, did everything they asked — and more — and they praised me. I learned that if you work hard, do things right, people will like you.

My teachers obviously liked me. The neighbors liked me. My friends liked me. And my life seemed to smooth out. When things were better for me, I also felt better physically.

At this time there was a lot of drinking going on at home, but the attitude was that drinking was normal and anyone who didn't drink was abnormal.

I didn't think much about it. I had other interests, other pre-occupations. I found ways to keep busy. I started taking pictures with my Brownie camera and putting them in scrapbooks. I bustled around doing housecleaning, laundry and ironing to help my mother.

Then there were school projects and church activities. I grew up Catholic, and the church played a very big role in my life. I loved the structure of Catholicism, the consistency of it. The church taught me trust and predictability. Later in life, some of my early training came to seem rigid. Yet in the early days, the church provided a haven and planted an enduring belief that God would be the most consistent factor in my life.

I could handle the days. I knew how to fill the hours. The nights, however, continued to be frightening. When my parents came home angry after an evening of drinking, I could hear them bickering and yelling in the kitchen or in the bedroom.

"I don't care what happens!" my father would yell, as they quarreled about money, about family problems or about sex. But I wanted so much to believe that everything was okay — that we were one big happy family day and night — that I never told anyone what I heard.

Even if I heard doors slam and furniture fall heavily to the floor, even when I found my mother weeping on the couch — I pretended not to see or hear.

The next morning life would go on as if nothing had happened.

Yet inside I was terrified. What was happening? I was overwhelmed with feelings of loneliness.

Why Doesn't Anyone Tell Me What's Going On? What's Going To Happen?

During the day I had lots of fun with my dad and my brother and my sister. Especially Sunday afternoons. We went for drives to visit neighbors and to see the countryside. We went on picnics, played horseshoes, joked, planted a garden, played the piano and sang songs.

I didn't have much fun with my mom. She always seemed to be working or tired. But I loved her, and I helped take the pressure off her at home by doing housework, cleaning, helping with the cooking and other chores.

I tried to make her happy, tried to make her proud of me. And I always went to my mother for solace and comfort. She met other needs, too. There was very little money in the house, and my mother kept a band-aid box with silver coins for all my emergencies.

I had fun with my dad, I felt secure with my mother — and all the while, I felt so lonely. I had no one to tell my feelings to.

Teen Years

When I was 14, my family suffered a severe crisis. My father's business was destroyed by fire. Our whole existence was threatened. Money had been scarce enough in the few years before the fire but after the fire, the family income looked hopeless.

I was terrified. No one was talking, no one was trying to lessen my fears. Mom and Dad talked with each other but they didn't tell me anything.

"Don't worry," they'd say. "Don't worry."

"Don't worry." I would lie in bed and wonder whether we would have enough food. Would I ever get to go to college now? What would happen if my parents had heart attacks from the strain and worry of this crisis?

"Don't worry." I worried about everyone — my parents, my brother and sister, my grandma. I wanted to help and I didn't know what to do. I felt guilty for being another burden. I felt angry because other kids seemed so secure. It wasn't fair!

I cried myself to sleep night after night. But I never told anyone about my worries and fears. Daylight hours were for making people happy.

Becoming A Family Princess

I hit upon a way to help the family, to mitigate the crisis and, at the same time, to become less of a burden. I'd become financially independent.

I found jobs. I worked for my father — did bookwork for his business. I also did bookwork for a gas station. Whenever I could find the time, I took baby-sitting jobs.

I paid my own expenses. And I bought things for members of my family. I bought clothes, toys and books for my brother and sister. Once I bought my sister a red sweater set, and was so proud of how cute she looked. I tried to buy the extras for our home.

Financial independence relieved some of my guilt, but my contribution was so small that I continued to feel inadequate.

At the same time, I noticed changes in my father. He started leaving home at 5:00 a.m. to open up his business. At around seven, he would give me a ride to school. I could smell alcohol on his breath when he picked me up. But I never mentioned it to anyone.

After school I would stop to see him at work, just to say "Hello" and to see if he was okay or if there were errands to do. Almost always I could smell the alcohol.

In the evening Dad would often go to sleep on the couch. The rest of the family moved in stony silence through the house.

The changes I saw in my father increased my fear. He didn't talk with me as much as he used to. He didn't seem interested. There were few jokes, very little laughter and no joy at all. The music had gone out of our lives.

Dad seemed angry all the time — angry and grouchy, like a wounded bear. Fearful of his temper, I told him only the good things because he might lose his temper and blame me if everything in my life wasn't just so, wasn't perfect.

I feared my father, yes, and I also felt sorry for him. I thought maybe he drank because of the fire. Or maybe it was because of the war — World War II. He went into the service when he was still suffering from the effects of a car accident. He was in combat in Germany, got wounded in action and had a problem with his leg that lasted for years. (As a small child I used to walk down to the river and throw flowers in the water, truly believing that my father would get them in Germany.)

Or maybe Dad drank because of his hard life growing up as an orphan. I felt he never had a chance, and that life had treated him unfairly.

I decided to make up for the losses, failures and set-backs he had suffered. He deserved more out of life, and I would see to it that he got the respect and recognition that he deserved.

I wrote to *This Is Your Life,* a popular television show hosted by Ralph Edwards. Each week a guest of honor listened to a stream of warm recollections from people in the past who really cared. Long-dead memories were stirred, old friendships were renewed — and everyone could see that the guest of honor was a worthy person. It was just what my father needed.

I was desperate. I wrote an 18-page letter begging the producers of *This Is Your Life* to select my father to be a guest of honor. I waited with high hopes. But as the weeks went by without a response, my hopes faded. I never received an answer, not even a form letter expressing regret.

No matter. If *This Is Your Life* wouldn't honor my father, I'd honor him myself. I'd make him proud — so proud of me. And if he was bolstered by pride, then maybe — just maybe — he wouldn't have to drink.

I worked harder at making friends and collecting honors, friendships and honors bestowed indirectly upon my father.

I won two state oratory contests.

I was president of four high school clubs: Library Club, Future Homemakers of America (FHA), *Spotlight* (School Newsletter) and Girl's Athletic Association (GAA).

I was an honor student, a member of the honor society.

I received the American Legion award, given by the American Legion to the high school student who demonstrated leadership, integrity, accomplishment, trust and commitment.

And I was a homecoming princess.

What honors for Emil! Relatives would come from hundreds of miles to watch as Emil shared his daughter's honors — to watch Sharon, homecoming princess, ride triumphantly down main street with a retinue of homecoming royalty.

My father would be so proud, I thought. We'd laugh and talk together once again. And the drinking? Ah, yes, the drinking would . . . go away.

By the time I got home from the homecoming parade, my father was celebrating my accomplishments — celebrating with booze. And within an hour, he was drunk and passed out.

I was pained, angry and disappointed. I felt helpless — helpless and thoroughly humiliated. That night I cried myself to sleep without changing my homecoming gown.

And what about my mother during these years? My relationship to Mom was full of anger and guilt.

I was angry because she didn't work things out with Dad. Maybe if she were different, he'd be different. Maybe she was putting too much pressure on him. Maybe she didn't give him enough love. Maybe . . . maybe . . . maybe.

At any rate, I was getting tired of being Miss Perfect, tired of having so much responsibility. I worried about who was going to take care of Dad when I left home.

Would she try to make him happy? Or would they just fight and hurt each other? Anger swept through me as I thought about Mom. And then I would be filled with guilt and remorse.

How could I be angry with someone who was obviously suffering so much herself? Mom worked so hard — she had to put up with so much. And through it all she took such good care of everyone. I was ashamed of the bitterness I had felt toward her.

But I also decided that I didn't want to be like her. I didn't want to be the kind of woman who worked hard for everyone else and took nothing for herself. I didn't want to be a patient, uncomplaining person. I wanted something out of life myself. But I felt guilty and selfish about meeting my own needs.

As usual I kept all these feelings inside. No one will understand, I thought. Besides I had my image to protect — my image and the image of my family.

It was hard to keep my true feelings and thoughts to myself. Once in a while I would slip. Often when company came to dinner on Sunday, the grownups would carry on long conversations as we ate. As I grew older, I began to have my own opinions and ideas on a wide variety of subjects. When I expressed my ideas, my dad would disagree. It wasn't the disagreement that hurt, it was the sarcasm he showed, the disrespect, the put-downs. Sometimes he would insult me and belittle me. If I fought back, he got angry. If I cried, I was accused of being too thin-skinned, too sensitive.

I never shared my feelings with either of my parents alone. Most of my outbursts took place at the Sunday dinner table. If my father disagreed with what I said, or if my words displeased him, he would retaliate by insulting and embarrassing me. Then I would feel humiliated and end up in tears. No matter how hard I tried to hold them back, the tears would come.

"You're nothing but a cry-baby," my father would say. "You're too thin-skinned. Can't take a joke."

Sometimes I fled in tears to my room. Other times I would be forbidden to leave the table, and I sat silently weeping before a plate of cold food.

Only once did I dare to speak back. "It isn't fair!" I cried. "It isn't fair for you to insult me just because I have feelings! I think that's wrong, and I think you're being cruel when you make fun of me whenever I say something. You think you're being funny when you ridicule me — well, it isn't funny!"

And only once did my father ever slap me. I stood in shocked disbelief. Here was the man who

loved me . . .

hugged me . . .

protected me . . .

taught me to drive . . .

taught me to do bookwork . . .

taught me to dance . . .

Here was the man who took me to ballgames and sang when I played the piano . . . and he slapped me because I dared to tell him truly how I felt.

I learned a profound lesson about how to cover up my feelings with those I loved. I learned that it was dangerous to be honest about my feelings.

And increasingly, emotional pain was becoming a part of my everyday life. It was no longer the nights that hurt, no longer the nights alone that were filled with fear and loneliness, with worry and pain. My emotions churned day and night.

14

Young Adult

I wanted to leave home, wanted to find a way to escape the growing turmoil. Yet I didn't dare go. Who would take care of my family if I left? But I was graduating from high school — that made it acceptable to go. Most of my graduating class were leaving to get jobs or go to school. Graduation resolved my dilemma. It wouldn't be acceptable to leave if I wanted to, but it was acceptable for me to leave because everyone else was doing it.

Four days after graduation, I left home and moved to a city 100 miles away. It felt good to be away during the week. I was very old for my years. When I look back, I sometimes feel as if I were born adult, a grown-up somehow absurdly encased in a child's body.

Away from home, I was capable and found it relatively easy to manage my own life Monday through Friday. For the first year I went back home almost every weekend to make sure everyone was all right.

Right out of high school I went to work and was able to get a pretty good job as a secretary because I took with me a lot of bookkeeping and shorthand and typing skills from high school. I felt the need to take care of myself and somehow get established. I bought a car, rented room and board, and had a salary coming in. It gave me a sense of stability to know I could financially take care of myself. A paycheck also gave me a great deal of pleasure to be able to buy things for my family. I remember buying a copper dining room light for my parents and some special clothes for my brother and sister.

Those years were filled with trying to make it better. I also belonged to a dance club, took voice lessons, belonged to a bowling team, worked as a volunteer for the Big Sister organization . . . and I found time to go out on dates two or three nights a week. Not a single person in my Monday-to-Friday life knew about the family turmoil that ensnared me, entangled me from a distant 100 miles.

I led two lives for Sharon, and my secret life was every bit as covert as the undercover life Herbert Philbrick led for the FBI. I had my pride and self-worth to protect. But I paid a price in weariness, in physical and emotional debilitation.

And there was more guilt. I felt guilty about my independent life, ashamed of enjoying the pleasure of dancing or bowling. How could I be out having fun when my family was in pain? Prayer, trust and hope were all that kept me going during this time.

My family appeared to be getting along well — on the surface, of course. But I could sense the tension, the old familiar stress and hints of pain. Tight lips, sharp glances, strained smiles and lackluster cheerfulness — all contradicted my parents' earnest assurances that everything was "just fine."

Everything was not just fine. But I didn't push it. I was so in need of relief myself that I wanted to believe in the facade, I wanted to take the pretense at face value. I was too tired to probe — too tired and too wary.

I was also enjoying my first real taste of freedom. But my pleasure with new-found freedom turned out to be short-lived. I began to feel guilty once more, guilty about the worsened conditions at home, and the impact on my brother and sister. I knew from the outstretched arms of my little sister that she was lonely for me. My brother's stuttering and the tears in his eyes told me that he was hurting and needed comfort and a haven.

There was an overwhelming sense of deterioration at home. The house needed attention and repair. My mom's once beautiful flower gardens were overgrown with weeds. The paint was chipping off the house, and the house itself seemed to be wearing out. The roof leaked, the drains clogged with increasing frequency, the ancient wiring was dangerously overloaded.

My mother was aging rapidly and suffered frequent, often inexplicable illnesses. My father wore a glassy-eyed vacant look, as if he were mesmerized by a vision of a bleak and joyless future.

Each time I returned to the city, my father wept and told me of his love for me. I will always remember him, tears streaming down his face, as he waved good-bye from the front porch.

I started getting sick when I went back to the city. Terrible stomach pains. High anxiety. Finally I was hospitalized with acute abdominal pain.

After peering and poking and probing and running many tests, physicians made a diagnosis: physical and emotional exhaustion. I spent several days in the hospital and when I was released, I was ordered to spend two weeks in bed.

Bed rest. That's what the doctor ordered. Naturally I spent most of the time thinking about my family. I resolved that I would try once again to make things better. "Only this time it will be different," I told myself. "I will take better care of myself."

A small, still voice in my head timidly asked, "How?"

I ignored the voice. "I will be strong and I will make things different for my family," I told myself, building up a hollow kind of confidence.

The small still voice persisted. "How? How will you make things better, Sharon? Are you really sure you can handle this?"

"Of course I can," I muttered. "I will just have to work harder and try to keep from getting emotionally involved."

Brave words. Perhaps I should have listened more closely to that small voice. I just continued trying.

15

Marriage

Within a year after my graduation from high school, I started dating an older man. To me he represented stability, normalcy, financial security and a haven, some kind of haven that would feel safer for me than my home.

I became engaged, and my parents made plans for the grandest wedding our community had ever seen. All the relatives on both sides of the family were coming.

There was a sense of gaiety surrounding my wedding plans. There was fun and laughter once again — music, food and animated conversation.

Maybe things would be like they used to be. Maybe our lives would be close once more, and all the fear and guilt and anger, all the unhappiness and insecurity would vanish like a bad dream. I felt excited and I was filled with anticipation.

My father bought cases of liquor for the wedding party. I begged him not to serve it.

He looked at me in sheer disbelief. "What kind of wedding party is it that doesn't serve liquor to the guests?" he argued.

But I was firm. "I won't come to the party if the liquor is served," I told him. I did not want my wedding to be spoiled, as I knew what would happen after the liquor began to flow.

We made a deal: no liquor during the day — only in the evening at the party. A small but important victory for me. It ensured at least that the wedding itself would not be spoiled by my father passing out as he gave the bride away.

I asked for help from a friend who hid my car in her garage. After the wedding, and before the party began, my husband and I made our getaway. I knew that it was more important for my father to serve liquor than it was for me to be at my wedding party.

Wife And Mother

My time was now taken up with new roles: a wife, a social butterfly and a homemaker. I soon became pregnant for the first time. I felt good about my marriage, good about imminent motherhood. My mind was filled with exciting plans and preparations. It was a stimulating time, a sunny zestful time.

I found that I made friends easily and enjoyed social life. I was congenial, good-humored and cheerful. It felt good to build a new life. I appeared happy and enjoyed having fun and meeting interesting people. But no one really knew me well.

Sometimes I'd go home for holidays or birthdays, but I began to go home less frequently, and I put more and more energy into my own life. I devoted my time to making a home away from home. After all, my home now was with my husband. I loved my new home, my own space, my friends.

Yes, it felt good to be away from my family. All the guilt and shame I felt about leaving my family was buried deep inside me. I was excited about being a mother and giving birth to my son. I knew immediately, that I wanted to be able to give something to this child, some laughter and some security. I didn't know how much I myself needed what I wanted to give my child. I wasn't aware of that at the time. My early marriage years were filled with all the things that creating a home calls for.

When my son was a baby, six or seven months old, I felt that since he was their first grandchild, my parents deserved some special time with him. We went for a weekend, but I decided we'd spend the whole week. It had been a long time since I had spent any more than a weekend with my parents.

I immediately regretted my decision to stay a whole week. All my worst fears of earlier years were confirmed. My father drank constantly. He didn't appear drunk — didn't stagger around, didn't slur his words or laugh long and raucously at inappropriate times, but he had that old familiar rigid, glassy-eyed, vacant look. My mother was sick and she cried a lot, even though she tried to hide the tears. Her face was tired and drawn. She looked aged far beyond her years.

My father was mean and insensitive to my brother. There were familiar insults and put-downs again, only this time directed at my brother. My brother was trying to act like a growing young man, cool and indifferent. He'd shrug and pretend it didn't hurt — yet I knew that it did. I could see and feel the pain in his eyes.

My little sister was a bundle of nerves. She was shy and uncommunicative. When she did speak, there was a tension and anguish in her voice.

Three days went by — only three days — and I couldn't stand it! I wanted to pack up my baby and get out of town as quickly as possible. In desperation I called Donald, a friend with whom I had gone to school. I begged him to come and get me and drive me and my son back to the city, back to the safety and sanity of my husband, my own home.

It was in the middle of the night, but my friend said he'd come. Very quietly I began to pack my clothes and my baby to sneak out of my parents' home. I had to get away undetected because I knew how much my father loved me and his grandson. It was a strange kind of love because my father couldn't tell the difference between love and possessiveness. Everything and everyone he loved had been taken from him — his mother abandoned him, his father died an early alcoholic death, his business burned and was a total loss.

I knew my father would never let us go.

I quietly crept down the stairs when I saw headlights outside. As I was going out, the baby started to cry, and my father appeared almost instantly.

He ordered me to stay. "If you take that baby and leave now," he warned, "you'll never be welcome in this house again!"

I tried to tell him how I felt, but he wouldn't listen. He had been drinking. He was hurt and angry that I was so afraid. He screamed at me. He told me I had broken his heart if I truly believed that he ever meant to hurt me or the family.

As he screamed at me, I screamed back. "Can't you see what's happening to everyone? Mom's sick. My brother's confused and has no one to turn to. My sister's a nervous wreck. I just can't take it any longer!"

My sister now peeked down from the top of the stairs. My brother was on his way down to help me. My father grabbed him and threw him down. My mother was there sobbing, and my son was screaming in my arms. It was an ugly scene. I thought I would go crazy.

I ran for the waiting car, ran as if I were fleeing for my life. Then we were on the road, away from the madhouse, away from the family. We drove 50 miles in silence, and then acting as if nothing unusual had happened, I asked my friend to stop at a phone.

I called home to check on my family. I was afraid my father, enraged by my flight from home, might lash out at the ones I'd left behind. What if he killed my mother? What if he blindly lashed out and killed my brother and sister?

Thinking these horrid thoughts increased my guilt, but I couldn't help it. My worry was real, and I needed to know if my family was still alive.

My mother answered the phone and relief surged through my body. She told me not to worry. I apologized for being such a problem for them. I was sorry, I said. Truly sorry. I hung up in tears.

This was my turning point.

Once a tower of strength and determination, I was beginning to crumble. I was weary, burned out . . . I was no longer the family caretaker. I was no longer the one who'd fix things so that the problems would disappear.

I was fast becoming the family problem myself.

From Special Caretaker To Problem

I became pregnant again. In the first three months of my second pregnancy I was very ill — sick enough to be bedridden most of the time. I suffered from migraines and ulcers, as well as anxiety and depression — now easily recognized as stress-related disorders. There were times I was so incapacitated, so physically rundown, that my doctor had to examine me at our home. I was simply too weak to go to his office.

My mother discounted my infirmity. "You don't know what being really sick is," she'd say, as if she had cornered the market on authentic illness. Of course, Mother was always sicker and more in need of help than I was, so I kept quiet about most of what was happening to me. I tried to avoid contact with her, because each time we got together, each time we spoke, a resurgence of guilt swept over me.

My solution? Draw back, Sharon, draw back from the family. I couldn't handle the turbulent emotions generated by my parents' demands, by my father's drinking and my mother's chronic infirmity. I needed a respite from pandemonium. Once again I pulled away from my family.

It helped. But about once every three or four months, I would cry. A release, a release of pain, fear and grief. Quiet tears at first. Then huge wracking hysterical sobs. Eventually the tears would stop, or the family physician would give me a shot that would put me to sleep and end the weeping. Then I would be strong again . . . for a while.

My daughter was born in the fall of the year. Another time of excitement: A grandaughter for my mother and father! Just the thing to help reconcile the bad feelings between my father and me.

My mother and father planned to visit us and the two grandchildren for Christmas Eve. All day we waited eagerly. Then it was evening. They were late. Something had to be wrong. They had called early in the morning and confirmed that they were coming. But my mother's voice was low, strained and guarded. It was the kind of voice that came during a big family fight.

As time slowly crawled on, Christmas Eve lost its rosy glow of cheer and fellowship. The carols, the baubles and the wrapped gifts seemed ominous, foreboding.

About 7:00 p.m. my uncle called. He simply said, "Your dad died. He was a good man. It wasn't his fault. Come home."

My mind went numb. Dead, I thought. Impossible! He's only 46 years old. He can't be dead! Must be a car accident.

I left my babies with friends and began the 100-mile drive to my parents' home. I expected to find my family and their car wrecked along the road. I didn't.

As I pulled up in front of my parents' house, I saw a bedraggled Christmas tree in the front yard. I was to find out later that in a fit of anger my father had thrown it out of the door earlier in the day.

Dazed, almost like a zombie, I went in. Tear-filled voices came at me in a jumble, and I pieced together fragments . . . Dad was drunk that morning . . . family fight . . . noon . . . mom, brother, sister . . . had to get out . . . went to visit relatives in the afternoon . . . Dad . . . alone . . . committed suicide . . . must have been afternoon, late afternoon.

The words began to jell in my mind. Dad, drunk and alone, had committed suicide. I heard the words, but I didn't want to believe them. I wanted Dad to come down the stairs and put his arm around me and tell me that everything would be all right.

Everything was not all right, and it wouldn't be for a long, long time. The next ten days were filled with tumult, with horror, shock and grief, with anger, hurt and fear — and above all, confusion and the nagging thought that if only I had been there . . . if, if, if . . .

Family Caretaker Returns

I mustered up the strength. I comforted my sister and brother. I helped my mother. Helped her clean out my father's business papers. Helped her write thank-you notes to friends and relatives. I went with her to open my father's safety deposit box and found that the house and cars, which had once been paid for, had been secretly mortgaged by Dad for drinking money.

I mustered up strength. I kissed my father good-bye in the coffin. He was wearing the navy blue suit he bought for my wedding. I ran my fingers through his curly black hair — the hair I had loved so much as a child. I studied his face.

Familiar, so familiar, but I would never see it again except when I see the family resemblance in my image in the mirror or when my son laughs and holds his head a certain way. "There's Dad," I say to myself. "There's Dad."

I was in control throughout it all, the detailed arrangements, the funeral, the aftermath. I hurt, I grieved inside. But I didn't cry. Sharon shed no tears for her father. After ten days I went home, home to my babies. I was afraid that my old family life would drag me away from my new family, that old family ties would sap my strength and take me away from my new friends.

I told everyone, "My father died of a sudden heart attack."

"Yes, it was a great shock. A great shock."

I didn't know how to take care of myself. It never occurred to me that I needed to be taken care of. I stayed in control when I went home to my husband and children. But I was afraid my old family life would take away my new family and was terrified that I was going to lose my children.

Caretaker To Problem: II

My life was crumbling. I was swamped with work and demands. My two babies needed a good deal of care, energy and time. I was just 24. My closest friend was the same age and she was dying of cancer.

My husband wanted my time and energy as well. He urged me to let go of my family of origin. My attention belonged to him and the children, he told me. My new family needed all of Sharon, not a fraction of Sharon left over when she had time. My husband and family needed a healthy, vibrant Sharon, not an ailing Sharon, not a distraught wife and mother full of nameless fears and anxieties.

I felt torn and pulled and pressured. Then another call came from home. Six weeks after my father's death, my mother herself was on the verge of death with a bleeding ulcer. I was called home again. Sharon would take charge.

During the next few days I made arrangements for Mother to have surgery. I helped my brother and sister get set up in alternate living arrangements. I scurried around the house, making sure it was tidy and secure and that the lights and water were shut off. Then I returned back home to my babies.

I cared for my children during the day, and made the 150-mile trip in the evening to be with my mother until she got out of intensive care.

I was drained, and felt myself getting sick again. The emotional numbness was returning. There was a growing sense of dread. I was desperately afraid of loss and anxious about my own guilt. There was a bitter irony in love, I thought. Love? If you love something, it will be taken away.

My children. My husband. My mother. My best friend. I loved them all — would my love bring them unhappiness? Would it end up killing them? I was frazzled and vulnerable, flooded with anxious thoughts, worries and even superstitions when it came to those I loved.

I was afraid my mother would die, that my children would get hurt, that my house would burn down. I dreaded the thought that I would get ill.

"If I get sick, who will take care of everyone else? Who will do what needs to be done? Who will do Sharon's job?"

A few short weeks after my mother's surgery, my best friend died. I sat up comforting her husband all night. We were all so young. She hadn't even got a start in life and had left a two-year-old son.

I went to the funeral home the next day to say good-bye. I returned to my own home and started to cry. This time I could not stop.

Deeply depressed, I cried for days. I could no longer escape, could no longer run, hide or cover up. I could no longer pretend "It will be all right."

This time I knew "It will *not* be all right."

I could no longer muster up strength, I couldn't be strong. This was my bottom. *I could do no more . . .*

I was hospitalized for depression, but refused medication. Tears were relieving, a kind of blessed relief. I did not want to stop crying.

I wanted to stop hurting, thinking, feeling, trying, struggling. I wanted to stop living.

Fortunately, I remembered my grandma (one of my angels) saying, *"There will be times in your life when you need to put your right foot in front of your left foot and keep going and you will come out of the fog."*

I tried to get help. There were two psychiatrists who told me to forget about my alcoholic family and get on in life. I attended some early Al-Anon meetings and was told I didn't belong there because I wasn't married to an alcoholic. In the sixties Al-Anon was much more rigid than it is today. I tried to get into 11 alcoholism treatment programs in Minnesota and was told they had nothing for someone who lived in an alcoholic home — only programs for the alcoholic, the addict or the people married to them. There was no help for me in my home state.

On Becoming A Choicemaker

As I hit my own emotional bottom, as I considered suicide, I knew that something had to change or I couldn't survive. After what seemed like an eternity of weeping and grieving, I surrendered to the one constant source of strength and hope that I knew to be real. I asked God to take me into his care and somehow put me back together again. I prayed and prayed. And I waited. I surrendered and continued to wait.

Part Four
Miracle Recognition
(Go With the Flow)

M y healing began with the waiting. Events and people began to come into my life. *The Miracle* started.

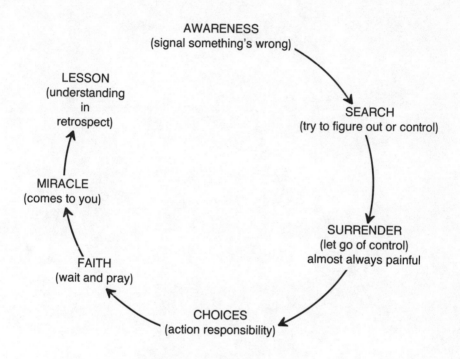

Figure 7. Spiritual Journey

16

Awareness

Awareness can be started by a variety of circumstances. Maybe it's something specific like an accident, a drunk-driving arrest, an intervention, a divorce, a child in trouble, loss of a job. Or maybe the awareness is a slow-growing restlessness, depression or state of anxiety that says something's wrong.

One day I became aware that I was very unhappy and there had to be something more. I had thought this at different times but now I felt it in such a way I could no longer ignore the message coming from within me. When I really became aware of how unhappy I was, I not only became afraid, I panicked. The fears and pain that I felt at this time were profound. My awareness led me to a search.

The first *awareness* came to me while I was at a dinner party. Someone told me about a treatment center that would take almost anybody. With only a glimmer of hope I gathered up my courage and made a trip to this program hundreds of miles away. I spent life-changing time in an alcoholic treatment center that was willing to take an adult child from an alcoholic family.

While there, I learned some important *awarenesses*:

1. I was dependent and my drug of choice was caretaking and serious workaholism.

2. Most of the alcoholic patients I met were children of alcoholics with feelings and compulsions just like mine.
3. I could learn to make choices in my own behalf.
4. I was not a bad person, only a tired, angry, guilty person trying to survive a history of stress, crisis and lack of nurturing.

The Decision To Live

I decided to fight back. I decided to survive. This began the slow painful process of becoming emotionally honest with myself. I had to find out what my own needs were. Then I needed to be honest with others about my needs.

My needs! No more evasion, no more pretense, no more martyrdom. I had to take a look at what Sharon needed. This was new for me.

It was scary. Progress didn't happen overnight. Sharon had a great fall, and there were no king's horses and no king's men to put Sharon back together again. There was no magic fairy godmother who'd wave a sparkling wand and reassemble all the shattered fragments of Sharon's psyche. The process was instead difficult, painful and sometimes surprisingly wonderful and delightful. I did not always like it, but I slowly gained understanding and *awareness.*

My fog lifted when I went to a prayer meeting where several people had gathered to simply pray together. At this meeting there was a priest from a Catholic church back in Minnesota who said to me, "I would like to invite you to a weekend retreat, The Cursillo."

I didn't know what the word Cursillo meant. I came to know later that it meant *short course in Christianity.* In my numbness I went to the Cursillo weekend retreat. For me it was like entering another world.

My world had been so full of chaos and pain for so long that I had begun to believe that stress was normal. At the Cursillo weekend I was stripped of responsibility and given time to be with myself in an atmosphere where people were willingly and generously wanting to nurture me. It was a powerful experience. There were many new awarenesses.

I remember having the luxury of being able to listen to talks, people sharing their life experiences. I started to feel some of my own feelings that had been deadened by stress for so long. I remember at one time beginning to cry. (I didn't want to cry in front of people.) Yet I didn't want to miss anything that was happening. In my unreal world, I sat in a room full of 40 or 50 people, sobbing. I remember putting on my sunglasses, sincerely believing that they wouldn't know I was crying.

Later, I saw a video tape of one of the lectures given on that weekend. Here was this person sitting with a bright orange corduroy skirt and black sunglasses, highly visible in a room full of people. Yet I remember that day feeling absolutely and totally invisible, sure that no one would have noticed me. You see, the way I felt, invisible was normal.

I remember after two or three days of music, laughter, nurturing and space to feel, that I lay down on my bed crying so convulsively that I was embarrassed. I remember getting off my bed and turning the water on in the shower so people couldn't hear me sob. I prayed, *"Dear God, I didn't know there was anything worse than the pain and the stress that I have been living in. Dear God, I do not know how to help myself, but I surrender. If you can help me, I will follow wherever I feel you take me."*

There was a sense of peace, a sense of comfort. My *awareness* was that *there is another way.* One can leave the depth of pain and the feeling of despair and one does not have to do it oneself. One has to really be ready to listen, to feel, to follow, to ask for help and to let others in. I remember coming out of that room with absolutely no sense of direction, other than to watch and wait. But I was aware. *There is another way.*

About three weeks later, I was approached by the diocese where I lived. I was asked if I would be willing to take an active leadership role in helping put on Cursillo types of retreats for other people and I said, *"yes."* I didn't know how and I didn't know what was expected. I only knew that I was going to follow for a while whatever was put in my path.

I began three or four years of directing spiritual retreats for people going through lifestyle changes, who were exploring their reality and beginning to search for some kind of spirituality or higher power concept outside of themselves. It was a wonderful three or four years. I shared many, many things, made new friends and continued to be *aware* that there was a lifestyle different from the kind of pain that I was living in.

By now my marriage was almost a repeat of my original home life. My husband didn't drink, but the rigidity, the blame, the anger and sarcasm and put-downs were no different than what it had been like for me in an alcoholic family. I felt very alone in my marriage. I also felt frightened. I felt totally responsible for my children as I watched my husband be emotionally unavailable to them.

In addition to my own pain, I began feeling the pain of the children. I loved them so much. Feeling emotionally abused by my husband felt normal to me, but it felt so unfair to my children.

My husband and I had joined a couples' group in our church. There again I found many new *awarenesses*. It was in this group that I began to listen to other people's stories and ways that other people had lived and how they had coped with family issues. I watched how the husbands and wives listened to each other and began to find new ways. They seemed to learn from the pain that they were in. They changed to make things better. That didn't happen in my marriage because my husband resisted any change. He absolutely refused to become a sharing part of the group. He refused to hear anything said to us.

While things were not working for me and my marriage, I did see that things did begin to work for other people. My *awareness* was that sometimes it's too late to recover with the person who you are with. However, there was hope to see that other people could get better, could resolve conflict and could have hope and joy in their lives.

After the four years that I spent putting on retreats, I decided to go back to school. Going to college had been dismissed for me when my family lost all of their finances through the loss of my father's business. I had been told during high school that going to college was just going to be out of reach. I had always been good at school, and had often regretted giving up a four-year college scholarship and going to work instead. I knew now that I needed to learn more. My *awareness* that things *could* be different challenged me to know more and more about *how* they could be different.

I went back to the University of Minnesota and majored in communications. While I was majoring in communications, I also continued my work doing retreats.

I loved school. I had won many awards in high school as a public speaker, and I found that learning in college was easy for me. It was also wonderful to be in an environment where I could think and feel and not feel controlled or oppressed as I did at home. This was another *awareness.*

In my third year of college, someone introduced me to another program in the state of Minnesota, a two-year program in chemical dependency. With all that had happened in my family and losing my father to alcoholism, I was very excited to know that there was a place to go to learn about this subject. I transferred into the two-year program and became a certified alcoholism specialist.

That two years became a continuation of my treatment. I learned about addiction. I learned about family systems. I learned about what had happened to me and what had happened to my father. But more importantly than anything I was learning academically, I was learning that I could make friends, that people liked me, that I could share myself. And I found that I could laugh. The only time that I laughed was when I was outside my home. This was a time of major new *awareness.*

Yet as well as I was doing at school, I could not make growth changes at home. I became afraid. The fear was that if I continued to grow, there were going to have to be many changes and I could see that my marriage was in serious trouble.

I continued my double life, experiencing more and more outside my home. At home I loved my children, loved being with them. I tried to be fully there for them, but was in tremendous pain because of the crisis my marriage was in. It was during this time that another major *awareness* was coming upon me.

It was a profound awareness. Maybe, just maybe, I didn't have to live in pain forever. I had met people at school and in the spiritual retreats who had divorced, and even saying that word felt awful to me. The idea of divorce for me felt like failure. It felt like sin. It felt like betrayal. Once in a while I let the word creep into my consciousness and my new awareness.

After I finished with school and became an alcoholism specialist, I decided I needed to finish my four-year degree and maybe get a master's degree. I kept right on going. Academically, it felt like I was in school all the time.

I did finish my four-year degree and did go on and get a Masters. While I was doing all of this, my life was splitting down the center. I was tremendously depressed. I was tired most of the time. My days consisted of full-time student, full-time mother and full-time wife. Two out of the three were healing and good for me but one was much too painful. It was hard to go on from day to day. Finally one day I said, "This is it." I filed for divorce.

I had talked many times with my husband about wanting a divorce. He simply did not believe that I ever would go through with it nor would he even talk to me about it. He refused to go to any kind of counseling.

One day I recognized how long the marriage had been dead.

Divorce! "My God, you don't really mean you're going through with it!" One of my friends had gasped in disbelief. Divorce was the kind of thing you might think about, you might ponder it or even casually mention it to a friend. But it wasn't something that a conventional young woman did — it just wasn't proper!

What was proper? It was proper to stick together for the children's sake. It was proper to stick together for security. It was proper to endure a relationship that was in pain because it was humiliating to admit failure in marriage.

Yet I went ahead with the divorce.

My mother rejected me for taking such a drastic step. My children reacted with baffled anger and resentment. My friends let me know clearly that they disapproved. Yet I went ahead. I did not want to stay married for my mother's sake or for my children or for my friends. I felt this was the first major life decision I had made for myself, and it brought me more pain. It was an important decision.

Over the next few months and years I learned I could survive. What an *awareness!!!* It did not feel like ending a marriage at all. I left with little emotion. I took my children and moved from my home and had an almost emotionless divorce. The only feeling I felt was relief.

I also learned that sometimes you know inside what is right and necessary. I was beginning to believe in myself and starting to trust my inner knowing.

There is a Zen saying: When the student is ready, the teacher appears. After I recognized that divorce was the right decision for me, it was some time before I could follow through and act on that decision. I simply was not ready to take action sooner. Once I was able to act and take the first major step of divorce, it became easier to take subsequent steps. I continued on in school and finished, and as I became ready for them, teachers and mentors continued to appear.

When the student is ready, the teacher appears.

The most difficult thing about being divorced was watching my children be traumatized by the change. They were very young at the time: 12, 10 and 8. They didn't understand. To some extent they had an abandoning mother who was spending a lot of her time in school. I worked as hard as I possibly could to build a nurturing home for them. In many ways I know I succeeded. In some ways I know that I failed. Out of all the things that I have done in my life, I feel that one I have done well was be a mother. My children were and continue to be one of the most important priorities of my life. But it was hard.

My husband refused to support us so we lived just a shade above poverty. But we made it. We also learned to have fun.

Most of the time, however, there was a sense of fear. There was fear that there would be no money, fear that I would be punished for getting a divorce, fear that I wasn't going to make it, fear that I was a bad person. But there was also some sort of clarity and peace within me ever since the day of surrender that said *SEARCH*.

17

The Search

I knew there had to be more and I began to find out what more really meant. There had to be other ways. People needed something else in their lives. Other people looked so much happier, as if they knew something I didn't. My search provided me with information, new ways of looking at things and new possibilities. My search became my drive and in that consistent drive for help, for change, for more, I was losing more parts of myself. I was tired, but I was not any more fulfilled. As a matter of fact, it was during this time that I really found out that *information without action leads to depression and frustration.* I was trying so hard and I couldn't get where I needed to go. I was starting to feel depressed and desperate.

Information without action leads to depression and frustration.

I began a serious *search* for me. Who was this person who skipped childhood, who missed out on the early years of learning trust, joy, spontaneity and self-confidence? Part of the process of change included professional treatment.

I was treated as a child from an alcoholic family system. It felt good to have someone hear how I felt for a change — how Sharon felt. And it felt good to have someone tell me I was okay. "Sharon is a good person." I liked the sound of it.

My first teacher appeared in the person of Gene Burke, a priest who facilitated a therapy group. I learned a great deal from him about "possibility." I had felt trapped for so long that I had grown to believe my helplessness—my powerlessness and my limitations. With Gene's support and encouragement, I began to act in my own behalf and feel good about it.

I continued my *search!* I started a job at an institute in Minneapolis, and I learned a lot more about addiction, about intervention and more importantly, I learned a lot about me. I learned that I did have skills and knowledge. I learned by sitting for many hours with other alcoholic families. I found I wasn't the only person who felt confused, bad or trapped.

While I was working at the institute and still continuing some of my Cursillo work, I was more and more aware of the needs of my children. I made a decision at that time to start a junior or a youth program for children. I wanted to bring the kind of unity, hope, learning and joy that we had for adults into a program for children. I talked to a priest in downtown Minneapolis who offered his church so I could start what I called the Friendship Club.

The Friendship Club was a program for kids from five to fifteen who were living in homes where parents were getting some sort of therapy. The parents were going to groups or coming to our retreats. Their children were usually left with babysitters, so the Friendship Club became an option. It was a place for kids to learn how to talk about their feelings, to bond with each other, to have some self-worth experiences and some joyful experiences for themselves. During the years that I worked with the Friendship Club, I honestly don't know whether they taught me or I taught them, or whether they gave to me or I gave to them. I have a hunch that in nurturing children, I was also nurturing myself. I was *searching* and I was learning.

During this time, I also joined a psychodrama group in downtown Minneapolis. Here I learned a tremendous amount about how it was possible to re-feel and re-experience past events in one's life and learn from them and heal from them. I took classes. I went to conferences. I read books. I made eleven trips to Esalen in Big Sur, California, studying everything from dance therapy to Gestalt to more psychodrama. I continued to *search*. I learned a tremendous amount in those days about various forms of psychotherapy. We're talking now about the 60s and 70s. I met many people who were going through some of their own private revolutions and changes.

At this time, I started a group in Minneapolis called *Search For Meaning*. These were people from different walks of life who were confronting much of their past history and traditional ways of doing things. We met on Sunday nights, and people began to share their experiences personally and professionally about what was happening in their lives and together we just *searched*.

These were my years of looking and trying and *searching*. They were wonderful years of learning. Yet for me, the *search* in itself became another complication. You see, I didn't know that what I really needed for myself was treatment. I didn't know that I didn't have a good sense of boundaries or know how to save energy for myself. I didn't know that I was carrying a tremendous amount of hurt and pain from the family I came from. I didn't know that I was *searching* for something OUTSIDE of myself to heal INSIDE wounds. I didn't know that it wouldn't work.

So while I was making all the efforts to *search* and to try to learn and to experience, I literally was wearing myself out and avoiding my continuing pain. I took everything that I had learned and began to give away to others before I began to take for myself.

———————————————•———————————————

*I took everything that I had learned and began
to give away to others before I began
to take for myself.*

———————————————•———————————————

The first agency I developed was called *The Family Factory*. It was a wonderful place. The Family Factory was a place where children who came from alcoholic homes could come and share and talk and learn and be with each other. I had no money to start this kind of program, but I knew a recovering person who owned an H & R Block Income Tax building. He told me that I could use that building for my purposes, but I could only have it from April 15 until Christmas. From January 1 to April 15, the building would be used for tax business.

The Family Factory opened up, and soon we had over 300 kids in some kind of group. It was always with the condition that all groups stopped in December and picked up again April 15. It was a couple of years before the Family Factory found a more permanent home. After the tax building, we used the basement of a dental building.

It was while we were at the dental building that a Lutheran minister from Minneapolis called me and offered me a two-story home. He told me that if I would be willing to work without wages, the church would be willing to fix up a building on its property and I could move into much bigger headquarters. I was thrilled. We moved into the building and called it *The House*. The House was another major learning for me. Being counselor, bookkeeper, administrator, group leader, staff supervisor and seeing approximately 40 patients per week was a real burn-out lifestyle.

I trained my children to be group leaders, recruited interns from the University of Minnesota and also found some clergy interns. We had many different kinds of groups for dysfunctional families and children. It was a rich, rich learning time.

But once again, the one thing I was not taking care of was myself. I had remarried by this time, and I remarried another untreated adult child from an alcoholic family. He and I had many dreams about what we were going to learn, put together, do and offer to others, always skipping the part of what we needed for ourselves. In many ways in my second marriage I married "treatment" and so did my husband. We helped each other learn and we helped each other heal. For a while the marriage was a nourishing time. We were two untreated people, trying to help each other and share what they knew with others. We did the sharing with others quite well, but the part about treating ourselves was neglected. In the neglect of caring for ourselves, the marriage died.

Once again, while I was doing all these wonderful things on the outside, which had been my pattern through grade school, high school, college and my first marriage, my inside self was dying. I did not see it. I did not feel it. I did not know it. All that I knew was that most of the time I was tired, most of the time I was trying to hold things together and most of the time I was busy trying to accomplish something. All the learning that I had done, all the degrees that I had gathered, all the experiences that I put myself through, all the hard work that I had put in, somehow were not adding up to any kind of personal healing, personal satisfaction or bringing any measure of joy in my life.

18

Surrender

I needed to stop, needed to stop trying so hard. I began to listen to myself. I felt overwhelmed and at rock bottom. Mostly I felt unfocused and tired. Surrender was very difficult for me. For a person who was always an organizer and a trier and a doer and a fixer, to simply surrender was very painful. It felt like giving up.

Today I know the difference between surrender and giving up is very big. I needed to stop my own compulsive drive, which was what I used to medicate personal pain. When I stopped medicating my pain by staying so busy and trying so many things and learning so many things, there was nothing left to do but feel it. I needed to hurt before I could act. I think this was my dawning. *When the hurt gets bad enough, it is easier to make risky and hard choices.*

It felt risky to stop controlling or trying to figure things out. Yet it felt riskier to continue living as I was — tired and non-fulfilled. I surrendered. It was a surrender that said I had to stop trying, stop controlling and stop medicating my pain with my busy-ness and my efforts. It was tremendously terrifying.

If I stop, what will happen? If I let go, would everything fall apart? Would I lose everything that I'd worked so hard for? I really didn't know what the answers were going to be. I only knew I couldn't keep doing it all. It was at this time that I started doing less and decided to simply pray and wait.

When I stopped being busy, the terror absolutely set in. I felt as if I were losing ground, losing touch with my children, my job, my mate, with myself, yet I didn't have the energy to hold it all together anymore. Some days were just extremely long days with not much accomplished. What I remember most about this time was being unfocused, sort of feeling as if I was lost in a thick fog. It was at this time that I sought some private therapy for myself. I hurt. I remember crying myself to sleep many nights as one day blended into another.

For me the compulsion had been busyness, work and control. Now I let go of that. I really felt like I was shattering. I also began to see things the way they were and not the way I wanted them to be.

I accepted during this time that I had made a mistake in my marriage. I had married someone who really didn't want the same kind of lifestyle that I did, who really wasn't prepared to take the recovery journey with me. He had a recovery journey of his own and he wanted a different kind of lifestyle. The idea of a second divorce brought about a deep despair. To hurt myself, my mate, my family and my children one more time seemed too much. I felt like a really bad person. I stayed in the hurt. I didn't avoid or run. I just hurt. It was during this time that I found a treatment program for alcoholics that accepted me — a child of an alcoholic.

I had tried so many times before to get help. I had been to a psychiatrist. I went to some 12-step programs, where they told me that I wasn't welcome because my husband wasn't an alcoholic. I had tried a marriage counselor. I had found nothing to help someone who kept setting themself up in bad relationships and repeating old behaviors, self-sabotaging behaviors, hurtful behaviors, someone who felt guilty and bad most of the time.

When I went to the alcoholism treatment center, the director asked me why I had come. I tried to explain. I told him that I was so very tired from all the effort I'd made, yet so few things were working out for me. I didn't want to do to my children what had been done to me. I felt guilty all the time. I felt that every time I wanted to do something for me, I ended up hurting other people. I felt so selfish and so bad. Why couldn't I be satisfied? Why couldn't I manage somehow? Why did I feel like such a failure?

I remember the director of the treatment center saying to me, "Sharon, which one of your parents drank?" I looked at him and said, "Both." He told me, "What you're feeling is very normal. No one has ever given you permission to be happy, permission to seek what you need for yourself, permission to love yourself and appreciate yourself for what you do right. Instead, they've pointed to the little pieces of what you did wrong that are part of everyone's life. Why don't you come in? I think you've come home."

In my pain, I entered the alcoholic treatment center and learned that I wasn't unique, that I wasn't bad and that I had been a part of a disease that destroyed the self-worth of everyone around it. The disease of alcoholism stripped people of their choices and the feelings of normalcy, setting people up to feel that pain and stress were normal. I finally realized at a very, very deep level that I couldn't fix everything that had ever happened to my family. I couldn't go back a generation and make it different.

The most I could do was to heal me and then be willing to give whatever I could to those around me. I learned that my first debt was to myself to survive and to heal. That was a stage of making choices in my own behalf.

I couldn't fix everything that had ever happened to my family. I couldn't go back a generation and make it different.

19

Choices

When I got tired of hurting, I started making choices. Big choices. They meant risks and a change of lifestyle, but I knew that if I didn't, I would live in the pain forever. The early choices were the most difficult, because I had made so few real choices in my life. So many choices were made FOR me that just learning HOW to make a significant choice was a hurdle. In making my life-changing decisions, I learned the process of choicemaking, a gift I cherish in my lifestyle today. In choicemaking I learned that I couldn't control the results of the choices I made. During this time my transformation started as I surrendered to choices (behavior change) and faith (waiting for results).

---

*During this time my transformation started as
I surrendered to choices (behavior change) and
faith (waiting for results).*

I learned to be compassionate with myself. I began to re-see myself as a young fearful child, as a struggling teenager and as a desperate young adult. When I really realized the kind of frantic journey that I had been on just to survive, I had to make some very, very difficult choices.

Yet I knew that saving my life literally depended on new choices. I had to reduce the toxicity in my life, whether that was toxic people, toxic circumstances or a toxic job.

I did some very difficult things. I resigned from my job in Minneapolis. It was a job at a very prestigious place, but I had to leave the toxicity of that agency in order to really feel and recognize who and what I was all about. It was an agency that was built around the wants and needs of one particular person. It was an agency that abused its employees, including me. For someone who had nearly always lived on the edge of poverty, the idea of having a job with a regular income at a prestigious agency was attractive. Yet I knew I had to leave so I quit my job.

I went through a second divorce and in many ways it was more emotional and painful than my first one mostly because I could feel. I could feel grief and I could feel sadness. The man who I divorced was a good man. He had fathered my children in many more ways than their birth father. There was a deep sadness. There was also some concern that my children wouldn't understand because I was leaving someone who they loved. Yet I knew that I had to leave for me and for the little child, Sharon, who had never really made a decision on her own behalf before.

I made a decision to move several thousand miles across the states to a new area to start *My Life* for the first time. I was trying on adulthood, making choices and changes on my own behalf for the first time. I needed to set boundaries around myself and leave all relationships that took advantage of me, both personal and professional. I remember the day that I piled into my car, left all the people in my life and began to drive to another state to start all over all by myself.

20

Faith

I didn't know what the results would be when I made the choices I had to make. I could only wait at this point in faith and prayer and see what happened. For someone who had learned to control outcomes, protect self and manipulate circumstances, this time of waiting was extremely hard. It required prayer, meditation and a conscious effort to let go of control. Little by little events "out of my control" began to happen. The miracle started to unfold.

Little by little events "out of my control" began to happen. The miracle started to unfold.

This time felt like being suspended in space. This was the time of faith. It was the waiting time.

Often it seems as if this is the space between trapezes. It is the faith leap when you leave something secure, yet you don't know if you will be caught. Part of me was frightened, and part of me felt the most centered and relieved that I can ever remember feeling. There is a tremendous inner peace when you give up control. For once there was nothing I was trying to make happen. Each day I felt I had time to see whether the sun was shining, whether it was clouded over or raining. I had time to be aware of everything that was going on around me. I worked, but it was working without a hurried fever pace, working without a goal, working without a plan, simply doing the work that was in front of me *one day at a time*. I was aware that I felt a bit aimless, but not unfocused. My focus was on learning to live one day at a time. And each day seemed quite long, quite full, but it was truly a time of "faith."

21

The Miracle

Things began to come to me in thoughts, ideas, creativity and people. I saw that the end result of letting go — surrendering and waiting — is the beginning of a miracle. For me, there was a learning to recognize *The Miracle* of my life. Later I realized that I was learning the process of "miracling." In transformation, miracles are occurring with great frequency. I call all of these miracles the process of "miracling." We can learn to recognize them in our everyday lives. Out of each miracle seems to emerge a lesson.

In transformation, miracles are occurring with great frequency. I call all of these miracles the process of "miracling."

A major change had taken place with my family back in Minnesota. With the help of other professionals, I had arranged an intervention with my mother. One of my greatest joys was when my mother asked to be taken to a treatment center for her addiction. I also went into treatment with her as her child — an adult child of an alcoholic.

The healing between us was miraculous. I have a deep sense of pride in my mother — pride in the courage it took for her to go through treatment, pride in her determination to recover from her addictions. And I have pride in her ability to let go of the past, to take each day as it comes.

One of the difficult problems I've had to face over the years is that just as the child fears the parents, the adult child fears authority. As I tried to bring my personal experience to my work as a professional, I met with a great deal of rejection. Working with families was outside the mainstream of psychology and social work, on the far fringes of social services. After all, the argument went, there was an "identified patient" to deal with—the alcoholic or chemically dependent person. Once the alcoholic was "fixed," the family would run good as new. In a sense, the identified patient was a lot like a faulty carburetor—a malfunctioning mechanism that could be overhauled or even replaced — without affecting the performance of other parts of the car's engine. The analogy was a mechanical one, over-simplistic and insensitive to the organic interconnections in a family system.

It was a long lonely struggle to try to bring family systems theory to bear on family problems in chemically dependent families. Professionals balked and treatment centers complained that they had all they could do to deal with the alcoholic, much less the family.

Recovering alcoholics were afraid that they would be reminded of the old pain in the family. They didn't want to become aware of unfinished family business because it would be another stress to deal with in recovery.

Spouses and family members didn't want to see themselves as being part of an illness system. It was the other person who was sick, who was the "identified patient." Spouses and family members were reluctant to seek their own therapy, reluctant to make changes. It is always more comfortable to believe that the alcoholic or drug-dependent person is at fault.

Children, too, wanted to avoid. They were tired of continued chaos in the problem-centered family. Kids found their own survival in fantasy or outside the family. They simply didn't want to feel the hurt, guilt and anger that came from facing their own roles in family hassles.

Because so many children of alcoholics become attracted to helping professions, many untreated adult children are in professional positions offering services to the chemically dependent or their families. Adult children are conditioned in youth to giving service, taking care of people, trying to figure out relationships and trying to understand themselves and others. Naturally, then, they gravitate to caretaking professions — to nursing, teaching, counseling, psychology, medicine, clergy and so on.

Untreated for their family illness — scarcely even aware that a family can be afflicted — these adult children in the helping professions still suffer from their own resistance to the family illness concept. To accept that information fully would be making an assessment of self, would be admitting that the helping professionals themselves have wounds that have not healed. It would mean admitting that even professionals themselves need help in dealing with the family issues growing out of the family illness of chemical dependency.

Fortunately recent developments have made it easier for helping professionals to recognize their adult child status. At the same time it has become more acceptable for helping professionals to take steps to resolve their own unfinished business.

In February, 1983, Joan Kroc invited several people to the Kroc ranch in Santa Barbara to discuss the needs of children of alcoholics. Along with several of my peers in the field, I came ready to share my expertise, experience and knowledge.

As we introduced ourselves and began talking about the gut-level important events that had shaped our lives, an unusual intimacy developed among us. We had come together as virtual strangers to one another, and in our uncannily similar experiences, we discovered we were soul-mates. We had the kind of instant understanding that's extraordinarily rare and precious.

The meeting had an indescribable quality of holiness. Members of the group who attended the meeting at the Kroc ranch became the founders of the National Association for Children of Alcoholics (NACoA).

On my way home from the meeting, I reflected on what had taken place the past few days. I wrote a letter on the plane to my new NACoA friends and colleagues. It read:

NATIONAL ASSOCIATION FOR CHILDREN OF ALCOHOLICS

Front Row left to right: Cathleen Brooks, Tim Allen, Tarpley Richards, Barbara Naiditch, Mary Brand. Second Row: Sharon Wegscheider, Bobbie Hodges, Jael Greenleaf, Robert Ackerman, Phil Diaz. Third Row: Robert Subby, Patricia O'Gorman, Timmen L. Cermak, Julie Bowden, Herbert L. Gravitz. Not Shown: Stephanie Brown, Claudia Black, Ellen Morehouse, Charles Whitfield, Joseph Kern, Rokelle Lerner.

Dear NACoA Friends,

As a child who grew up in a family suffering from alcoholism, I have struggled with the fear and mistrust of feeling a sense of belonging — of joy and hope. As many of you know, my father died an alcoholic suicide at the age of 46. My mother suffered for years with pill and alcohol addiction. They were warm, wonderful people and parents. It was the alcohol that devastated our family.

I spent half a lifetime in what felt like struggle — too many ways to mention here. There were highs and lows, losses and gains — but never much relief from the feeling of struggle. What was constant through all this, however, was the ability to feel a Higher Power and to know at some level that I belonged as a child and servant of that power. The hope and joy was transmitted through people caring, and that care has nurtured and sustained me. Each of you reading this letter knows who you are and your relationship to me.

Through people and my Higher Power, I have accomplished some things I'm proud of. The births of my three children were events of total ecstasy to be equalled only by the intensity and commitment I felt in their growing years.

As I sit on the plane flying from California to Texas, I am allowing myself to experience the awe and humility I feel right now. I feel that the birthing of NACoA and its need for commitment and nurturing are important values for me and for each of us.

In the speed of what has happened in the 48 hours just behind us, I was a "good CoA" (Child of an Alcoholic), full of task and purpose. It is only now — alone — that I am flooded with feeling . . . As I look down on the mountains, it feels right. I'm flying high. What my tears are saying for me is,

"I am honored that you want and trust me with the role of chairperson for your national organization — one that I believe will make a difference in the world of alcoholism and addiction. I sincerely feel 'joy, hope and a sense of belonging.' To serve and work with the caliber of people who sat in on this historic formation meeting was enough good feeling to last a long time. To be able to continue in a role of trusted leadership is an honor.

"I pledge to help each of you expand in whatever way you want, with respect to serving the organization. And I will share with you whatever talent and gifts I have in order for us to work together as a collective body of people 'who care.' Together we will bring hope to thousands who still feel 'crazy and alone.' "

Sharon

Today NACoA is a mainstream organization, and concerns about children of alcoholics have led to what can only be described as a broad-based social movement. It involves educators, physicians, the juvenile justice system and other workers, who for years had been baffled by what seemed to be inexplicable behavior in children and adults alike, behavior that has turned out to be closely linked to being raised as a child in an alcoholic family.

Being a part of the founding of NACoA was one of the miracles for me. By this time I was beginning to establish a consistent faith that miracles would happen. This faith was built on the foundation of my childhood beliefs.

Always I had known at a very deep level that God loved me. By now I had learned that my family loved me the best they knew how. I learned to ask for help when I needed it. I also learned to love unconditionally, and that feels wonderful.

The Miracle

During my time of waiting, during my time of faith, a man came into my life. I had met him before, but we had never really talked or exchanged very much about our personal lives. During this time of waiting, we became friends and out of friendship grew love. This man eventually became my husband. At our wedding we read a prayer I'd like to share with you now, because it really tells our love story.

> Love is a friendship that has caught fire,
> It is quiet understanding, mutual confidence,
>   sharing and forgiving.
> It is loyalty through the good times and bad.
> It settles for less than perfection and makes
>   allowances for weaknesses.
> Love is content with the present, it hopes for
>   the future and doesn't brood over the past. It
>   is the day in, day out chronicle of
>   irritations, problems, compromises, small
>   disappointments, big victories and common
>   goals.
> If you have love in your life, it can make up for a great many
>   things you lack. If you don't have it, no matter what else
>   there is, it is not enough.
>
>   Author Unknown

There was the good news and the bad news about our coming together. My children love Joe. They were eager to see me happy and that was good news. There were people in Joe's life, personal and professional, who did not welcome me. I don't know exactly how they saw me, but it must have been as some sort of interloper. Our first few years were full of struggles.

Thank goodness, both of us had learned that in letting go, seeking help, asking for help and waiting to see what happens, one is given strength. We selected a therapist, a man named John, who became almost a third leg to our relationship in our early years. He helped us sort and plan and plough through pain.

Day by day our relationship grew stronger and stronger. *The Miracle continued to unfold.* It is wonderful to rest, to be quiet, to feel a close bond with a person, a kindred soul, where honesty and intimacy can flourish in an atmosphere that encourages continued exploration and growth.

Perhaps this quiet inner peace is what I've been searching for since I was a little girl, looking for a way to feel safe, looking for a place to be safe. I have found what I sought — the way, the place and the safety.

And I bring the message to others—to co-dependents and children of alcoholics of all ages: Full recovery does happen. It is not easy. It does not happen by itself.

Risk, change, belief in a Higher Power and an outstretched hand to other people — all these can indeed lead to a sense of comfort, safety, warmth, love and fulfillment.

I know. I have traveled the road. And it's been worth every mile of the journey, one day at a time.

———————————————————•———————————————————

Risk, change, belief in a Higher Power and an outstretched hand to other people — all these can indeed lead to a sense of comfort, safety, warmth, love and fulfillment.

———————————————————•———————————————————

During the early days of NACoA, hundreds of us gave each other mutual support and encouragement as we explored thoughts and feelings—as we learned that we were, in fact, more alike than different. We learned that we weren't crazy and alone, that we weren't odd creatures full of bizarre emotions and wicked thoughts. We had normal feelings, given our tension-filled and shattering life histories. And we learned that we could become open to change and transformation.

I began to be able to separate the disease of my parents from the people my parents were. With that ability, I became able to separate my behaviors and illness from who I was. I began to love and respect myself in a new way.

The way to accept myself fully and grow to love myself has truly been hard at times. Hard? At times, it seemed well-nigh impossible. During the years, there have been many more hurdles.

My relationship with Joe was a growing value and priority. I felt I had met my "soul-mate." Yet it, too, presented pain. It was clear that his co-workers and children did not accept me as his partner. I felt judged and discounted. Yet with our mutual friends (personal and professional) we received much support. We made the decision to marry.

The Wedding

At our wedding, my brother, whom I had not seen or been close to for many years, came to offer to give me away. It was a wonderful healing and our relationship has continued to grow. My mom was there and gave me her blessing. My children were there and gave me support. Joe's father and siblings also came to the wedding and gave blessings and love to both of us. *The Miracle unfolded.*

Joe and I made difficult decisions but decided to move from where we were living and go to a part of the country that neither of us had ever experienced before. We have found in the heart of the United States, in the Native American Sioux Land, a city called Rapid City. It is nestled in the beautiful Black Hills of South Dakota. I had been told many years ago by Virginia Satir that it was a holy site and that the hills were filled with spirit. It was not until I visited there that I found out how true that was. Joe and I moved to the hills to begin to make our personal and our professional home. *The Miracle unfolded.*

It seemed that once we had settled in the hills, the gifts continued to come. We have found people who care about people. We have found nature that nurtures and creates serenity. We have found a sense of spirituality that neither of us had ever known or learned. We have found our spiritual home. We believe the living miracle is to be shared. We have created a vehicle in the hills through treatment and training and workshops. It is a vehicle to continue the unfolding miracle.

We have learned that miracles are not a one-time event. Living the miracle is to allow one's life to unfold and respond at every possibility. It's to respond to each person and each event with compassion and understanding, love and touch. No, a miracle is not a one-time event. Living in the miracle is a lifestyle.

Living in the miracle is a lifestyle.

The Miracle has continued to unfold. We have been blessed with growing attendance at our programs in the Black Hills. Watching "The Miracle" unfold for so many has reinforced our own decisions. There has been much family healing and today we feel blessed by so many who love us and support our work.

To begin to understand miracles is to begin to be willing to look at hard times, at pain, at grief and still not give up faith. It's being willing to look for the lessons that come from living through the pain. Many years ago people found reassuring proof that there was a God by being able to share their stories of miracles. Just our human bodies alone are miracles. It's a miracle that our digestive systems and our skin and our eyes and our built-in defense mechanisms work. Our hormonal systems, our chemical systems, our feelings, all of these things work with very little awareness on our part. They just simply work because we work and that in itself is a miracle.

When we look at the phenomenal capability of the body, the emotions and the soul to re-frame, re-examine, re-feel, re-create and re-heal, we are made aware of the "miracle" of each one of us. Each miracle brings with it a "lesson in living."

22

Learning

The lessons go on during all of life. The first lesson I learned was that the miracle of recovery is an ongoing process. It started with an awareness and grew into a lesson. It goes like this:

There were many years of fog-living with much confusion and pain. Today as I re-frame my history, the miracles jump out at me. With this knowledge I feel much more confident about today and have very little worry or concern about tomorrow. Lessons add up to wisdom and we begin to find joy, serenity and understanding in our lives. New awareness keeps coming to us and feeding the cycle.

Part Five
Lessons

23

Family Of Choice

Each painful relationship serves a purpose. The person who enables the alcoholic is needed to pick up the pieces and protect the alcoholic from the consequences of drinking. The workaholic needs someone to handle the day-to-day responsibilities so that time can be spent in excess devotion to a job or career. Because each person in a dysfunctional relationship serves a purpose, change is threatening. Painful families do not want change. They want things to remain the same. The first person in a "couple" or "family" system to make healthy choices will often be in trouble with the family.

Painful families do not want change. They want things to remain the same.

During the time of early recovery it is important to develop a safety net of friends. I call this safety net a *Family of Choice*. One needs to make four to six good friends who will support your growth and change. It is important that these friends be people who have grown and taken necessary risks in their own life. We often reinforce our own stuckness and fears by choosing friends with similar problems. Misery loves company, and often friends are chosen simply to share problems and struggles.

We often reinforce our own stuckness and fears by choosing friends with similar problems.

To support recovery and growth, seek friends who can role-model the kind of life and relationships you want to have.

The process of choosing spiritual mothers, fathers, sisters, brothers, daughters and sons does not eliminate blood relationships. It simply means that sometimes blood family members cannot or will not fulfill relationship needs. Because of illness, resentment, addiction and many other reasons, mothering, fathering, sonning and daughtering do not happen. This is also true of brothering and sistering. We can become stuck in a pattern of waiting and hoping things will change. However, doing the same things over and over with the same people, expecting a different answer, is a clear form of insanity.

Doing the same things over and over with the same people, expecting a different answer, is a clear form of insanity.

When we do not get our needs met from members of our blood family, we can choose to move out of the old pattern of expecting a different result. We can choose to form other relationships. It is healthy and good to develop relationships where one can get these needs met. Sometimes we can afford to give more to our blood family members when we are getting our needs met through our family of choice. The process of "family-ing" is one we can all learn and celebrate.

24

What's It All About?

One can ask the average person, "What's most important to you? Your job and the things you do outside of the home or your relationships, your mate and your family?" Almost everybody will say family. But then watch how people live. It seems very often that the largest investment of time, energy and money has a whole lot more to do with people's careers than it does with the relationships they live in.

We often ask our clients or patients, "Is what you do really what you want out of life?" The answer they most often report is, "I want to be healthy and in a loving relationship." Then we explore the way they actually live. They are frequently polluting their bodies with all kinds of toxic substances (alcohol, drugs, nicotine and excess sugar). They keep their lives busy to avoid closeness and warmth in their relationships. Yearning for satisfaction and inner peace seems to be as much of a struggle in today's society as it ever was. So often we are too tired and fragmented to develop close relationships.

---

*Yearning for satisfaction and inner peace
seems to be as much of a struggle in
today's society as it ever was.*

When we live out of sync or harmony with what we call our values, internally we will remain restless with a never-ending hunger and thirst. This hunger and thirst is often what propels a person in choosing certain values to honor and a certain lifestyle. It is this hunger and thirst that many describe as their quest to understand more about "spirituality." Spirituality is our sense of wholeness and satisfaction. It's our hunger and longing for belonging and inner peace. Without a sense of our spirituality, we see many manifestations of our soul-restlessness:

CRAVING	OUTCOME
Hunger	Eating disorders
Thirst	Alcoholism
Quiet	Drugs
Excitement	Drugs and frenetic activity
Belonging	Relationship dependency
Power	Workaholism
Acceptance	Sexual acting out

By spiritual, I do not mean religious in any formal sense but simply progress in goodness. I mean essentially the ability to love and the ability to experience and to respond with deepening sensitivity to the world in which one lives.

---

*Spirituality is the ability to love and the
ability to experience and to respond with
deepening sensitivity to the world
in which one lives.*

One simple way of understanding spirituality is to see that it is concerned with our ability, through our attitudes and actions, to relate to others, to ourselves, and to God as we understand God. All of us, addicted or not, have a way of relating to our own lives, other people and God in a way which tends either to be positive, healthy, fulfilling and life-giving, or tends toward the negative, self-defeating and destructive.

---

*It seems that the spiritual adventure begins
when we give up the search for certainty
and go on an adventure of discovery.*

Spirituality is a simple way of living. It seems there are four basic movements that recovering people need to make to put their lives on a positive spiritual basis. These are:

1. ***From fear to trust.*** As we build a support system, we learn we can trust others. As we grow and develop our relationship with our Higher Power, we learn we can trust ourselves.
2. ***From self-pity to gratitude.*** We can learn to re-frame our thinking to appreciate what we have gained from our experiences and how much we have been given.
3. ***From resentment to acceptance.*** We can let go of past hurts and learn to see those around us with compassion.
4. ***From dishonesty to honesty.*** We can acknowledge the reality of "what was" and "what is now," and we can accept our own responsibility for our growth.

So often we are taught answers to life's questions long before we are interested. As children and as young adults, we were taught values, theologies and answers. Yet our own personal lives had not experienced enough to formulate the questions we wanted answered. It's important to wait for the basic questions of life to arrive before we theologize — otherwise we have simple and easy answers, but no pressing questions.

---

*It's important to wait for the basic questions
of life to arrive before we theologize —
otherwise we have simple and easy answers,
but no pressing questions.*

In my own quest for understanding, I've come to imagine the spiritual journey as a companionship or walk with my Higher Power. It is a journey from insight, miracles and lessons to more insight, miracles and lessons.

So much of the struggle in life is that people do not intentionally escape into sick or painful behavior but rather are trying to find what we so naturally seek. We are looking for a flow *into* life, not an escape from it. A person who is troubled is often a seeker of a full life who does not know how to seek.

There is a life force that creates expression. When this expression is thwarted or stopped by people and circumstances, there is a natural painful frustration.

As we travel on our journey, there will be many teachers or mentors. We need not spend energy finding them. They will find us. As the Buddhist saying , "When the student is ready, the teacher will appear" becomes a reality to you, you will accept that EVERYONE in your path becomes a potential teacher or mentor.

---

*As the Buddhist saying, "When the student is
ready, the teacher will appear" becomes a
reality to you, you will accept that
everyone in your path becomes a
potential teacher or mentor.*

As we explore our reality and purpose, we find spirituality demands that we respond to an internal desire to move to a greater sense of freedom from what keeps us stuck and pain-filled. We acquire a freedom to take more control of our own lives. This is the thirst for freedom.

Love, freedom, risk and choice are difficult arts to master. Despite our deep need for these virtues, we often are diverted from fulfilling our dreams by devoting our time and energies instead to success, money, prestige, power, old hurts, current comforts or other family members.

But the soul is restless. It will speak to us with anxiety and inner conflict until it is fulfilled. Our spiritual attitude will be shaped at the point of conviction — when we are willing to define what we wish to live and risk for.

Our spiritual attitude will be shaped at the point of conviction — when we are willing to define what we wish to live and risk for.

Risks must be taken. Of course, merely to try is to risk failure. But not to risk is the greatest hazard to our own growth. Those who risk nothing, do nothing, have nothing. They may avoid suffering and sorrow, but they will not learn, feel, change, grow, love and blossom. Chained by certitudes, they are slaves who forfeit even in recovery their own freedom.

Only the person who risks is free, and only a free person can open the door to true spirituality and faith.

To expose feelings is to risk your true self.
To laugh is to risk appearing the fool.
To cry is to risk being judged a sentimentalist.
To reach out for another is to risk involvement —
     and hurt.
And to love is to risk not being loved in return.

To place your ideas and dreams before others is
   to risk their loss. And to hope is to risk despair.
But to not hope is to risk relapse into how it was
   before.

Adapted from an Anonymous Quote

Freedom is not measured, however, by the choices we made or the risks we took. Freedom is measured instead by the intensity of that moment when in our inner self we somehow knew that there was no going back. At these moments we break through, lifted to a higher level as we transcend the bonds of our illness. We are transformed into a fresh state of being, a heightened awareness and consciousness — and it only happens *one day at a time.*

Co-creation of our lives invites us into the spiritual journey. Life becomes a continuing state of new possibilities when we can see our efforts as "attempts to grow." Mistakes and failures become an irrelevant concept and self-shame loses its power in our lives. We understand our choices as our efforts. Our efforts lead us to lessons, and lessons show us how to live.

We see life as a journey and its events as teachers. We accept the role of co-creator. As co-creators we take on the responsibility to be as mentally, emotionally and physically available as possible to the process. As we release this non-toxic energy, we are free to truly unfold. This is a grand experience and the greatest high of all.

25

Forgiveness Is A
Gift We Give Ourselves

ɤ Dag Hammarskjold said it in 1956: *"Forgiveness is the answer
  to the child's dream of a miracle by which what is broken is
made whole again, what is soiled is again made clean."*

Forgiveness is a gift we give ourselves. It implies that we admit we
do not have complete understanding of an event or circumstances.
Forgiveness acknowledges that we do not have the knowledge or the
wisdom to sit as judge, jury and executioner over people who may
have hurt us in the past. *Forgiveness is a choice.* We choose life for
ourselves and others when we forgive.

1. We relieve ourselves of the burden of carrying around hurt,
   anger, pain and loneliness. Healing happens for us and we
   feel lighter and freer.
2. We give someone else the freedom to live their life (or
   sometimes rest in peace) and work out all their own
   behaviors, feelings and consequences in their own way.

Accepting how it was or is requires great personal honesty. We
sometimes tend to myth-make because it's easier. Seeing things as

worse than they were can allow us to avoid the risk of reconciliation. Feeling all the feelings and forgiving someone else is a gift we can give ourselves. It's called *serenity.* When we let go of the energy it takes to hold onto blame and resentment, we have the energy we need to get our own needs met.

When we let go of the energy it takes to hold onto blame and resentment, we have the energy we need to get our own needs met.

As an example of this, I'd like to tell you about Danny. Danny chose to come to one of our programs when he was only 12. He shared with us that he watched his older brother heal from anger and he wanted that for himself. He told about how he hated his alcoholic father. It was clear to him that when he was very angry with his father, he would start an asthma attack. Lately he had so much asthma trouble that he had to stop playing sports and doing certain school activities.

He said that all he ever really wanted was for his dad to hold him, say he loved him and let him know Danny was important to him. He said that Dad was sober now, but he hated him more than he did while he was drinking. He went on to explain that when Dad was drinking, he had a disease and couldn't make loving choices. Now that Dad was sober, he still didn't reach out and now he had choices. Dad replaced his alcohol with his recovery program, but life didn't change for Danny. He told us how he came home from school and was telling Dad about his fears of getting beat up. He was one of the smallest kids in his class. Dad just looked at him and said, "Easy does it, son. You've got to learn to let go of these fears." Danny said he wanted a hug and some understanding from his dad, not a recovery slogan.

Danny completed the treatment program and on the day he left said, "I found a lot of dads in this program and I got a lot of hugs. It's much less important to me that Dad doesn't know I'm alive and never touches me. I know now to ask for support from wherever I can get it."

Several months later I was out east at a conference, and Danny raised his hand from the audience and said, "37, Sharon." At break-time he came up to tell me he had been in his dad's arms 37 times over the past few months. When I questioned him about whether his dad was now hugging him, he said nope. He went on to tell me how at holiday time, his grandparents (Dad's dad) had come to visit. Danny watched Grandpa and Dad over the holiday. He told me, "I noticed that Grandpa never touched or hugged or even talked nice to Dad. No wonder Dad didn't know how to treat me."

With his abundance of treatment hugs and his new ability to get more, Danny had started hugging his dad. He told me, "Sharon, I found out an interesting thing. It doesn't matter who starts a hug — you make a connection with the other person. I'm going to keep giving my dad hugs until someday he learns and has so many, he can afford to give one away. I want to be nearby and get the first one."

Here's a young man who has learned to forgive and use his energy for getting his needs met. With fulfilled needs, he can afford to help someone else, in this case his father. He has learned to plant his own garden, instead of waiting for someone to send him flowers.

Instead of waiting for someone to send you flowers — plant a garden.

Examine those you have hurt and if possible, consider making verbal or written amends. If the person is not available, you can make amends through prayer.

If you would like to forgive someone to release both you and them, consider the payoff there has been in not forgiving. If the payoff is less important today, again use words (verbal or written) to forgive. Once again if the person is not available, forgiveness can be accomplished through prayer.

26

Picking The Scab Keeps A Sore From Healing

Often someone in counseling will do a cathartic piece of work around some traumatic event. The very next session, they will want to ask one more question or add one more piece of information and re-do the work.

Often resolution is frightening because it is new and unfamiliar. We become quite comfortable with our hurts, guilts and shames. Resolution, hope and relief are too new to give insight or comfort. Instead of becoming accustomed to the change, the tendency is to "pick the scab" to make ourselves sore and familiar again. Becoming comfortable with a healed self takes time and new experience. It is important to leave therapeutic work alone for a while.

Another way to say it is to tell the story of a frustrated farmer who rarely had a bumper crop. He could be seen every day pulling up the roots of his plants to see how they were doing and wondering why he was not successful.

Re-doing work that has already been done too often keeps us in a "wounded framework." It insulates us from the unfamiliar which is full recovery.

Take a risk — recover . . . .

133

27

It's Lonely At The Top

Workaholics are those people who feel as though their profession and their specific job is the most important focus in the whole world. I remember a lecturer on an airplane telling me, "When I first started traveling, it seemed exciting and glamorous. Today I know all about personal loneliness and the role is getting emptier. I would rather be loved at close range than worshipped from afar. I feel like a high-class hobo living out of a suitcase. When the lights go down, I'm really nobody." This is one who has learned that *doing* does not heal *being.*

Workaholism has many faces, but common features are appearing tired (especially around the eyes) and appearing sad (most suffer relationship loneliness).

CHARACTERISTICS OF THE WORKAHOLIC

1. Boring conversationalist (only talks about self and job)
2. Preoccupied with job and co-workers
3. Little time at home
4. Always reading and keeping up with work
5. Poor self-care (often overweight)
6. Eats fast

7. Anxious when on vacation
8. Less fulfilling relationship/sexual life
9. Reluctant to delegate
10. Feels responsible to keep producing and act on every creative idea.

Feelings of inadequacy are often the fuel that keeps our destructive behavior burning. Even though we may have accomplished great things, many of us are driven on to do more and more. It's as though we are striving to get the notice of some mysterious judge who will say, "That's good — you've done a good job and you've done enough."

THERE ARE MANY STYLES OF WORKAHOLICS:

1. **THE VOLUNTEER**

   This is someone who gets things done. They are dedicated to hard work and personal sacrifice.

2. **THE HOMEMAKER**

   Everything is centered around home and family. Meals, decorating, repair work, yards, etc., require constant attention. There are endless home duties.

3. **THE PARENT**

   Life is centered around the children. The children's needs come before everyone else, including the spouse. Holidays, vacations, finances and education are all focused on children's needs.

4. **THE SPORTAHOLIC**

   Any sport. It could be golf, tennis, football, etc., and can involve participating, watching or both. Being around a sport addict (active or passive) is a lonely place to be. Their preoccupation and compulsion interferes with relationships.

5. **THE PROFESSIONAL**

   Unfortunately there is not necessarily a connection between working hard and accomplishing much. Much workaholism is just "busywork" to look important and valuable. There is a payoff. Excess work can:

   1. Numb emotion
   2. Justify avoiding relationships
   3. Cover insecurities

4. Get appreciation from others to make up for lack of love
5. Get one noticed and liked.

It is important to stop excess work and spend plenty of time being good to oneself. We can say to ourselves — "You've done enough, now take some time for yourself — you are worth it."

Now is the time to make up for some of the missed pleasures and excitement of childhood. When we are aware of our responsibility to be good to ourselves, we will be committing to putting work in its proper perspective.

28

Workaholism

In the old days, the employee who came to work early and stayed late was considered "loyal and motivated." As extra projects were completed and new creative projects started, this employee would have been viewed as super-productive, ambitious and driven to succeed.

Today there is more understanding of the driven person. More information is teaching us that this person is probably plugging voids in his or her personal life. All addictions have similar roots, and workaholism acts like an addiction. There seems to be a base feeling of inadequacy and fear.

The workaholic tends to work to avoid loneliness, criticism or emotional pain in personal relationships. Eventually the world closes in on a workaholic and burnout takes place. Burnout is a step along the way to broken marriages, heart attacks, aborted careers, defensive withdrawal into half-led uncreative lives and even suicide.

BURNED OUT. The description scarcely could be more apt. The human flame that burns too brightly without refueling diminishes, flickers and goes out. People who burn out are victims of stress overload. They've worked too hard, given too much for too long and the ever-rattier rat race inexorably takes its toll.

"I don't care anymore." "I have nothing left to give." "I'm drained." "I'm exhausted." These are burned-out men and women describing their overwhelming internal depletion. Not surprisingly such emotional malaise puts them on a short fuse. They become negative and easily frustrated, and they find it increasingly difficult to deal with others and even themselves.

The burnout victim is chronically fatigued physically as well. He or she may have regular bouts of insomnia or even if able to sleep, rise in the morning more tired than refreshed. Colds may persist over weeks and months. Gastric distress is common, as are back problems, headaches and more serious stress-related illnesses.

Two types of people are most prone to burnout. First is the person who has a shaky sense of self to start out with, who depends on constant validation from others for self-esteem. Second is the somewhat pessimistic person who dwells on the negative aspects of each day's activities, instead of seeking out and focusing on the positive.

Burned-out people tend to build walls between themselves and others. Overburdened "helping professionals" cope with stress by holding themselves at an emotional distance from their clients and develop an aloofness both at home and at work.

What starts out as a self-protective device — building a buffer against excessive emotional demands — can evolve gradually into an alienation from loved ones in the middle years. It hits many workaholics at this point just how much they've lost. When burnout becomes advanced and turns into chronic anxiety or depression, then therapy and/or treatment is advisable.

To prevent or address early workaholism:

   1. **Learn to listen to yourself:**
       When tired — rest.
       When irritable — do something nice for yourself.
       When hungry — eat something good for you.
       When lonely — call someone or find another way to
           reach out.
   2. **Replenish yourself:**
       Find new pleasure interests.
       Spend time with hobbies.
       Learn something new.

3. Take time to foster positive physical health:

Eat a healthy diet.

Get enough exercise.

Get all the sleep your body requires.

Don't consume toxins (nicotine, drugs).

Use alcohol moderately if at all.

4. Feel feelings:

Do not stuff anger—learn ways to express it appropriately.

Do not stuff your hurt feelings—let someone know how you feel.

Do not stuff loneliness—acknowledge it to yourself as the first step toward relieving it.

Learn to recognize and accept all your feelings, both positive and negative.

5. Separate job from home:

Leave work physically at work whenever possible — don't carry a briefcase full of papers home every night.

Take a lunch hour away from your desk.

If you have to work at home occasionally, have a specific place to do that—don't work in bed, in the family room, etc.

Find other things besides work to talk about at home or with friends.

Become aware of the times you tell family members, "Not right now, I have work to do."

6. Give yourself time:

Take plenty of time to walk in the park.

Ride a bike.

Listen to music.

Visit a museum.

See a show.

7. Play:

Be sure each day has at least 30 minutes of play.

8. Pray:

Be sure each day has time for meditation.

29

One Day At A Time

Sam Hardy, a good friend, shared a wonderful story at one of our workshops. He told of being in an institution during his drinking days. There was a catatonic man in the group. For weeks the group shared life stories. Only the catatonic man didn't speak. When Sam started going to AA meetings, he took his friend with him. So far his friend had been totally silent. Yet each week Sam would pick him up, drive him to AA and then drive him home again. Many weeks later the catatonic man spontaneously spoke! His first words were, "The 12 steps would be a good way of life for anyone." I agree.

The 12 steps are used by Alcoholics Anonymous, Al-Anon, Overeaters Anonymous, Emotions Anonymous, Narcotics Anonymous and many other groups. When I first began my recovery, I heard Father Martin give a lecture that was extremely meaningful. He had paraphrased the 12 steps into what he called . . .

SHORTHAND FOR THE 12 STEPS

1. Saw a problem
2. Heard there was help
3. Decided to trust help the best I could
4. Took a good look at myself

5. Shared that "look at self" with another
6. Practiced trusting a Higher Power
7. Asked for help from that Higher Power
8. Thought about those I'd hurt (including self)
9. Said I was sorry whenever I could
10. Gave myself regular check-ups
11. Grew in trusting a Higher Power
12. Live these steps and help others when and however I can.

Father Martin also shared Dr. Bob Smith's brief summary of the 12 steps:

> Trust God
> Clean House
> Help People

Thanks, Sam H. and Father Martin.

30

Self-Worth:
The Bottom Line

Ways To Find Self-Worth

1. COUNT THE GOOD THINGS.

2. BE LOVABLE. We all need love but are we lovable? We can become more lovable by showing our interest in other people, being willing to connect, letting down our guard to become more vulnerable and approachable and allowing ourselves to have fun.

3. LEARN FROM EXPERIENCE. Especially from our mistakes — we can see them as opportunities to grow.

4. REMEMBER TO WHOM YOU BELONG. If you have survived much, then know you are a link in a chain of divine power.

5. BE COURAGEOUS. With Higher Power on your side, how can you lose? Take the leap. What's the worst that can happen? Poise brings harmony and allows God's work to be done. Face each situation fearlessly and each problem will fall away of its own accord.

6. KEEP FIT OR GET FIT. It's a great way to profit by time and helps us assess where we put energy. Pay attention to relationships and how they affect you physically. Often instead of saying, "What's the matter with you?" it's more accurate to say, "Who's the matter with you?"

7. TAKE TIME TO ENJOY. Don't hurry, don't worry, take time to smell the flowers. Serenity is never in a hurry. Ships come in on a calm sea. The two main robbers of our serenity are the past and the future. Serenity is not quick joy, but rather a powerful long-lasting inner peace. Its secret is acceptance of day-to-day living and the ability to live gracefully.

8. KEEP LEARNING. We can learn from everyone around us — peers, the elderly, the young, those we like and those we dislike. We can learn to follow our intuition and never violate a hunch, trusting our own inner voice to teach us what we need to know.

9. LIVE USEFULLY. There is always the need to see each other through. It's traveling together. When we are all in the same boat, it's rarely lonely. Only when we hold out with arrogance or self-pity do we suffer loneliness. Somewhere, somehow, somebody needs us, just us, no matter who we are or how simple the offering of help. There is a place that you are to fill and no one else can do it. One of my beliefs about regret is that, even if a wrong or regret cannot be righted, its effect can be neutralized by doing some kindness in the present wherever we can.

10. VALUE SIMPLICITY. Wise people are happy with small pleasures, but very little pleases silly and self-absorbed people.

11. WELCOME CHANGE. Nature's law is that all things must either progress or perish. To oppose change is to defy the workings of the universe. Change is a part of life.

12. LEARN THE IMPORTANCE AND POWER OF CELEBRATION. We are free. We need to claim this freedom. We cannot free ourselves in one area or from one influence and then accept a new bondage. Being caught up in pain can be a new bondage. Break the chain and claim your joy.

31

Recover Or Repeat

Serenity Requires Healing Past Relationships

"You don't get to choose how you're going to die — or when — you can only decide how you're going to live."

Joan Baez

We can choose our attitudes, and we can choose our actions and behavior. Where do we go from here? We no longer can look back and blame. We can only look forward and take responsibility. Our options are only limited by our vision and our willingness to risk. In the past we often opted for a passive life and ended up feeling powerless. Today we are free to fully participate in our lives and take action. It's time to be an actor — rather than a reactor.

Our options are only limited by our vision
and our willingness to risk.

In no way do I want to diminish the past. Rather, I want to face it, challenge it, forgive it, learn from it and move on. In the area of unfinished business in past history, we now know that we can recover. Following our personal treatment, we can . . .

1. Go back and share the pain and the feelings that have long festered. Then we can choose to say good-bye to either issues or people. This can be done in person or in psychodrama therapy.
2. We can also choose to forgive, to ask for forgiveness and then work on re-establishing relationships.

We have choices in recovery. Staying stuck, feeling powerless and postponing action are part of our illness.

In the past we may have hung on to yesterday's problems and pains. However, we have learned that focusing our concern on yesterday prevents us from being ready to grow today when "the teacher appears."

Life's events occur so rapidly that if we are still preoccupied and obsessed with the past, we miss the opportunities of the present. We can relish and even come to appreciate what we learned from the past, but then we can choose to let it go.

Life's events occur so rapidly that if we are still preoccupied and obsessed with the past, we miss the opportunities of the present.

Formerly there were really only two ways to approach life — as a victim or as a fighter. Many of us learned to react most of the time, and only as we started to recover did we become actors. Being the victim was familiar to many. Realizing we have choices is new — coming to know we don't have to let life happen to us, but we can make life happen.

It's hard, but it's necessary to choose behavior, friends, work situations and activities that please us and support our growth. That means we might have to say good-bye to behavior, friends, work situations and activities that feed our low self-worth or negative feelings.

The aim is full recovery. We will be challenged as we grow.

1. **THOSE WHO ARE USED TO OUR FRENETIC ACTIVITY AND WORKAHOLISM WILL BE A BIT MIFFED WHEN WE START TO CARE FOR OURSELVES.** Self-caring people refuse to be used and taken advantage of.

2. **THOSE WHO CHOOSE TO REMAIN VICTIMS AND ADVOCATES OF PERCEIVED VICTIMS WILL BE SUSPICIOUS OF THOSE WHO CHOOSE TO GET WELL.** They will sabotage recovering people every chance they get. Misery loves company!

3. **THERE WILL BE NECESSARY TIMES OF GRIEF.** In order to make room for new people, places, events and settings, other people, places, events and settings will need to go. Grief is a necessary and expected part of the healing process.

4. **THERE WILL BE TIMES OF SELF-DOUBT.** As we grow into a new way of being, health will feel different and unfamiliar. It will take time to feel comfortable.

Yet welcome the challenges. It is often easier for us to remember the darker periods of our life, periods when we dreaded the future, fearing it would just be more of the same. Fear and dread are still occasional visitors but we do not need to give them time or importance. We can choose to let them go as we become more comfortable with our many choices.

1. **WE HAVE THE OPTION AT THIS TIME IN OUR LIFE TO MOVE AHEAD WITH COURAGE AND DETERMINATION.** Recovery means going forth, fully hoping for joy and weathering the pitfalls. It means not avoiding the experiences or activities that we fear we can't handle. Only through our survival of them do we come to know who we really are and come to understand the strength available to us at every moment. And that is wisdom.

When we approach life tentatively, we reap only a portion of its gifts. It's like watching a movie in black and white that's supposed to be in technicolor. Our lives are in color, but we must have courage to let the colors emerge, to feel them, absorb them, be changed by them. Within our depths, we find our true selves. The complexities of life teach us wisdom. And becoming wise eases the many pitfalls in our path.

Living life is much more than just being alive. We can choose to jump in with both feet.

2. **WE HAVE THE OPTION OF FOSTERING ENTHUSIASM.** When enthusiasm is absent in our lives, we feel both apathy and fear that feeds on itself. Pray for the gift of enthusiasm and you will feel the energy begin to flow.

3. **WE HAVE THE OPTION TO RECOGNIZE AND KNOW THAT PAIN IN LIFE IS INEVITABLE BUT SUFFERING IS OPTIONAL.** Perceiving our challenges as opportunities for positive growth, rather than stumbling blocks in our path to success, is a choice readily available. What is inevitable — a matter over which we have no choice — is that difficult times and painful experiences will visit us.

We can, however, accept the situation, choose to learn from it and go on. No circumstance demands ongoing suffering. Of course, the hurt is sometimes there, but so is the growth from a hurting situation. Problems have only the size and power you give them.

We will never be free from all the difficulties during any period of our lives. But we have the personal power to eliminate the threat or the sting of any challenge. It's our vision of circumstances that gives them their interpretation.

At this moment, we are defining our experience. We are labeling events good or bad, valuable or meaningless. And our growth, particularly this day, is greatly influenced by the value judgments we attach to our experiences.

We can choose not to make mountains out of the molehills of life.

One of the gifts of recovery is spontaneity. Spontaneity in recovery means that we are finally free from old frames of reference. It's that moment of freedom when we can face situations, explore them and act in freedom without old emotional hangovers. We choose to let go of the old arguments, the obsessions with past relationships or the need for approval from people of the past. Then we are fully present for the surprises of each new day.

All of this may sound easier said than done. And yet as we practice the principles of recovery, we begin to relax — somehow starting to believe that better times are ahead. In time we will come to understand the part that a painful circumstance has played in our lives. Hindsight makes it so much clearer. The broken marriage, the lost job, the loneliness have all contributed to who we are becoming. The joy of the wisdom we are acquiring is that hindsight comes more quickly. We can on occasion begin to accept a difficult situation's contribution to our wholeness even while we are caught in the turmoil.

When we realize that we are free agents and not helpless victims, we can assume responsibility for ourselves. We can move from pain to choice.

No matter how your life is at the present, you have the power to change things for the better. There is help available. There is always a starting point. There is another chance if you are willing to take action on your own behalf. Once you have become a choicemaker, the opportunities are unlimited. LET THE PAST ENRICH YOU AND GO FORTH IN YOUR OWN RECOVERY.

————————————●————————————

When we realize that we are free agents and
not helpless victims, we can assume
responsibility for ourselves.

————————————●————————————

32

Step-Parenting: Would You Like To Join Our Family?

Many of the problems step-parents encounter are the same ones natural parents encounter. However, there is a tendency to think problems are different for step-parents.

The well-being of children in step-families depends a great deal on how adults treat each other. Hostility between ex-spouses makes life miserable for their children. Especially damaging is a position by one or both biological parents that the other is a "bad" person and not to be trusted or loved.

It's very important to remember that adults fall in and out of love. Children do not, and they certainly should not be expected to change feelings towards a parent. We need to remember that our children do not choose to stop loving a parent.

Putting a child in the position of having to take sides in akin to asking them to love the right side of their body and hate the left side.

It can't be done. Children must be given permission to love both natural parents. Only then will they be emotionally able to accept a new adult in a parental role.

Three basic myths occur in troubled step-families.

1. We are going to be just like the past family.
2. If we all try hard enough, there won't be any anger, hurt or sadness.
3. If we all live under the same roof, we will all love each other equally.

Step-parents who believe these myths are bound to be disappointed. Research shows that it takes between two and seven years to feel like a unit, that step-parents and step-children may never love one another — and should not be expected to — and that the nuclear family cannot be recreated.

Making the couple the top priority is absolutely essential to developing a happy step-family system. What makes this family unit most successful is for the two adults to love each other enormously and honestly. They must put each other first and then work out the problems with the step-children. Whenever the step-children are placed first, above the step-parents, the marriage is in trouble.

The couple bond must be nurtured because it is the most fragile of all the family connections and yet it is the one that determines the stability of the family. Couples who do not make time for themselves regularly are likely to find themselves part of the many second marriages that end in divorce.

Keep all the relationships in a step-family separate, especially the couple relationship. There are five specific stages to the step-family journey. The stages I have seen most often in my work have been . . .

1. **Hope.** This is going to be better and we'll all be happy.
2. **Disappointment.** It's not working out the way I thought it would.
3. **Conflict.** Who is going to win here? There is too much going on.
4. **Effort.** Let's just keep talking, negotiating and experimenting with this new way of living.
5. **Reward.** It's starting to feel better. If we each try to each give a little, we're probably going to work things out.

*To fall in love and make room for an instant
family is an act of faith, courage and
renewal. It speaks fully and joyously of the
strength and triumph of the human spirit.*

33

Humor Is The
Best Cure For Shame

Everybody experiences shame but part of the reason it has been so elusive in psychological terms is that it has been overshadowed by the study of guilt. It is also difficult to measure and harder to bring into the open than many other emotions that researchers study with ease.

Shame is the condition of feeling "not worthy" or having low "self-worth." While we are able to help our other emotions be released, shame is an emotion difficult to discharge. With hurt, we can cry. With anger, we can yell. With grief, we can weep. With joy, we can laugh. To release shame, we must change our behavior. When we take action in our own behalf, we lift the feelings of shame and begin to feel strength and pride in its place.

Shame goes to our core and basic sense of self and is experienced as embarrassment or humiliation. It requires us to re-look at where and how we missed out on validations that made us feel competent and worthy. When we have not experienced that our efforts matter, we feel inferior, inadequate and unlovable.

Beneath the self-adoring posturing of the narcissist, psychoanalysts say, is a sense of shame and self-loathing. Early and repeated childhood experiences that leave such people with a strong sense of being unlovable impel them to prove their worthiness with ever more impressive triumphs.

A sense of shame drives some people to build an inflated self-image through the pursuit of fame and excess amounts of money. The sense of shame leads them to become emotionally controlled and to set demanding standards for themselves.

Many believe that the single best antidote to shame is a person's ability to "lighten up" and be able to laugh at themselves.

Examples would be . . .

• Stories told at 12-step meetings.
• Telling jokes.
• Telling personal experiences.

Our biochemistry changes when we smile and when we laugh. Our body temperature changes, and the muscles in our face relax. As people take themselves less seriously and learn to laugh at circumstances, their shame will begin to lighten.

Behavior change will increase a feeling of manageability and safety. Recovery and growth is about making order out of chaos and then making new choices in the direction of self-worth.

Recovery and growth is about making order out of chaos and then making new choices in the direction of self-worth.

With these changes, shame is transformed into worth.

34

Advanced Recovery: Am I Finished Yet???

Knowing when we are in full recovery is a challenge. Do we need to keep learning new things, going to groups and going to conferences, or does the time come when we can just "do life?" Growth and change are a part of "doing life," yet there is a time when we know that the hardest intense work of recovery is over.

Some signs of advanced recovery are . . .

1. Lifestyle changes are made and new choices get easier.
2. We know when to quit growing and start expanding. We take in less information and spend more time devoted to action steps.
3. We make regular choices to nurture our self and others around us.
4. Intimacy and commitment become important values that we are willing to put time and energy into.
5. Increased playtime.
6. We find ourselves in healthy rather than toxic relationships. This is true both personally and professionally.

*Growth and change are a part of "doing life,"
yet there is a time when we know that the
hardest intense work of recovery is over.*

35

Choosing Health
Is A Healthy Choice

In co-dependency there is a high risk of having physical illness develop. The dynamics of stress left unattended can become "distress" and lead to stress-related illnesses.

Both men and women are subject to stress-related illnesses, but sometimes their different roles trigger different illnesses. Men often develop high blood pressure and ulcers. Women hold in their feelings and become depressed.

Many persons who have lived in painful high-stress families have suffered losses. The rules in high-stress families often prevent healthy crying and grieving. When we do not grieve in a healthy way, we act out our pain instead. Grief and anger may be a big part of depression, compulsion and addiction. It may even affect the lowering of our body's immune response which we need to fight off infection and cancer. Fear can result in anxiety and panic disorders. Guilt can lead to self-neglect, sexual dysfunction and other chronic conditions.

Dr. Charles Whitfield's article, "Co-dependency: Our Most Common Addiction," published in Wellness Associates, states:

"Preliminary studies suggest that writing and sharing our feelings strengthens our body's immune response, as shown by the following scientific study:

"Twenty-five adults kept a diary of disturbing life events for five days, and wrote how they felt about each of them. Another 25 adults kept a diary about superficial life events only. When their immune response was measured at six weeks, and then six months later, as compared with their baseline, the former group had improved immune response, whereas the latter group had no change.

"In my medical practice, which for the first few years involved mostly conventional, somatically oriented medicine — and then the last 12 years, which has been progressively an eclectically-oriented psychotherapy — I have observed numerous co-dependent patients. I noticed a pattern of chronic functional, psychosomatic or physical illness in these people, covering a spectrum from asthma, to migraine headaches, to arthritis, to hearing loss, all of which tended to clear with treatment that was specific for their co-dependency."

It's essential to feel what we feel and express it in order to maintain our health. One doctor, when asked how important he thought feelings were, said, "I tell all my patients to make their choices based on what would feel right if they knew they were going to die in a day, a week or a year. That's the one way of giving people an immediate awareness of how they feel, even if they have never paid attention to feelings. You don't have the luxury of five years of psychoanalysis if you may not live that long. You must begin change immediately."

Liking yourself profoundly influences the state of your body. The extent to which we love ourselves determines whether we eat right, get enough sleep, avoid toxins, (nicotine, drugs, excess alcohol) and get adequate exercise. These decisions control about 90% of the factors that determine our health.

We don't yet understand all the ways brain chemicals are related to emotions and thoughts, but we know enough to say our state of mind has an immediate and direct effort on our state of body.

Bernie Siegel, M.D., stated in an article he wrote for *NEW WOMAN,* March 1988, that we can change the body by dealing with how we feel. If we ignore our despair, the body receives a "die" message. If we deal with our pain and seek help, then the message is, "Living is difficult but desirable," and the immune system works to keep us alive.

In the same article, Al Siebert described the personalities of survivors. He listed the following indicators of the survivor personality:

- Aimless playfulness for its own sake, like that of a happy child.
- The ability to become so deeply absorbed in an activity that you lose track of time, external events and all your worries, often whistling, humming or talking to yourself absent-mindedly.
- A childlike innocent curiosity.
- An observant nonjudgmental style.
- A willingness to look foolish, make mistakes and laugh at yourself.
- Open-minded acceptance of criticism about yourself.
- An active imagination, daydreams, mental play and conversations with yourself.

If interpreted as a set of goals, this list may seem formidable, but these traits develop automatically from personal growth. Although personality change is hard, you can make each of these traits your own. There is much we can do to choose health —

1. Choose to put only nourishment into our bodies (not toxins or excesses).
2. Sleep when tired.
3. Allow feelings to surface.
4. Express those feelings.
5. Exercise regularly and joyfully.
6. Honor relationships.
7. Develop a sense of humor.
8. Develop faith.

I think of God as an intelligent loving energy or guiding light in each person's life. This God is a resource who gives us the tools we need to achieve our own happiness and well-being.

Choose health.

36

Big Deals
And Little Deals

Betrayal by a friend always hurts. On a beautiful day a letter came in the mail bringing the news that I had been betrayed by a friend. A friend had taken some ideas I had shared with her and published them as her own. I was hurt and then became very angry. My day was filled with little sarcasms about my friend, and I was preoccupied with my own hurt.

Later that day I received a phone call from another friend who shared with me that her husband had just been diagnosed with a terminal illness and probably would not live out the year. Immediately my incident about the betrayal was put into its proper perspective.

Many years ago I learned an important lesson about "What's really important enough to fret over." In the midst of my trying to complete an educational degree, manage a home and hold down a full-time job, I was often fretting about one thing or another. Then one of my family members suffered a debilitating illness. I needed to stop, assess and appreciate that the only true crisis is the threatened

159

or actual loss of life. They are the "big deals" — everything else is a "little deal." When I save my fretting energy only for big deals, my life is more serene. Most of the time I remember that. With my recent experience I was in need of being reminded.

———————————•———————————

*When I save my fretting energy only for
big deals, my life is more serene.*

———————————•———————————

37

Emotional Intercourse

V "I sure would like to have a more intimate relationship" is a common wish often mentioned. Yet the word "intimacy" seems so illusive. How do we find intimacy in our relationships and passion in our sex? There is a way to actually train ourselves to increase our ability to be passionate.

First we learn that . . .

1. **Emotional intercourse** is the sharing of all feelings. This means no medicating of these feelings with outside chemicals (alcohol, drugs, sugar, nicotine).
2. **Emotional afterplay** is the sharing of love and pleasure feelings (love, joy, trust, play, appreciation, respect, silliness, etc.).

To increase passion when you desire to couple, you follow these guidelines:

★ The first step is EMOTIONAL INTERCOURSE. Spend perhaps 20 to 30 minutes in sharing feelings.
★ Then arousal occurs and can be aided by touch.
★ This is followed by intercourse and orgasm.
★ Then, very important, is EMOTIONAL AFTERPLAY. This is another time-span of 20 to 30 minutes for sharing love feelings and closeness.

161

These steps increase passion to be held in reserve until the next desire for coupling. Over time there are more and more wonderful tender feelings to share. Both desire for sex and pleasure during sex increase because the physical intimacy is accompanied by emotional intimacy.

38

The Chase —
The Explosion —
The Shame

I Hurt Myself Again . . . .

When Beth, for example, wants to talk to Paul, she often follows him around saying in a multitude of ways, "Listen to me."

If Paul is not able to hear, does not want to hear or wants to punish or control Beth, he just finds ways to shut down, say no or walk away.

If Beth is not willing or strong enough to share her hurt and anger at being discounted, she will sulk. As her anger builds and builds, she will finally explode inappropriately in a rage or become hysterical. This gives Paul a chance to point out the ridiculous behavior Beth is demonstrating. Then she will feel ashamed (shame) and worse than she did in the beginning.

This process also works well, of course, if Paul is initiating the need to talk and Beth is doing the walk-away routine. It is a cycle

163

that can be part of any relationship between two people, whether they are friends, lovers or family members.

This is a form of self-defeating behavior. It's much healthier to be angry and express it right at the beginning.

It's much healthier to be angry and express it right at the beginning.

Then there will be no need for any explosion or accompanying shame.

39

From Feeling
To Defense

Feelings are wonderful clues that show us there is a situation to be responded to. Feelings need to be expressed and used as guideposts to operate in our day-to-day life. If we do not respond to our feelings and share them, they become character defenses and handicap us in relationships and interactions with others.

For example:

- Guilt not expressed becomes shame.
- Anger not expressed becomes resentment.
- Inadequacy not expressed becomes arrogance.
- Loneliness not expressed becomes dependency.
- Hurt not expressed becomes withdrawal.
- Sadness not expressed becomes depression.

Feelings expressed become the link between people. If both the sharer and listener are honest with feelings and care for the other person, their feeling sharing creates bonding and intimacy.

40

Divorce Is Not Just Between Two People

When the decision to divorce is made, many systems change, not just the coupleship. When both partners have agreed to a divorce, it's important that both come to an acceptance of the changes, and help themselves and each other make the transition with the least possible amount of pain. When a couple continues with anger, bitterness and vindictiveness, they are demonstrating that they are still emotionally tied together and the healing has not been completed.

Children Need Help To Cope With The Changes They Will Go Through

1. **First of all, it's helpful if children do not have to make extra changes** (school, house, neighborhood, etc.). If those changes are unavoidable, then minimize them wherever possible and use whatever resources are available to help children through them.

166

2. **Children will feel less tension if parents feel less guilt.** It's important for parents to remember that unhappy homes cause emotional unhappiness for children. The pain of divorce lessens with time for healing. Unhappy parents and homes are constant.
3. **Children must never be used to carry messages or communications for the parents.** It's the parents' responsibility to communicate directly with each other.
4. **Allow and encourage children to share all their feelings about the divorce.** Assume the children will have anger and hurt feelings and let them know these feelings are natural and okay to express.
5. **Let the children know they are not to blame for the divorce.** It's important to say this very clearly.

When a good friend or a member of a family gets a divorce, there are many awkward situations. How do you have two friends without taking sides? How do you not alienate anyone? To help a friend you might . . .

1. Refrain from criticizing them or the former spouse.
2. Still invite them as a single to an event where you might have invited them as a couple.
3. Call from time to time to offer support and friendship.
4. Ask them about their feelings and listen supportively.
5. Suggest some new ways to spend time together as your friend adjusts to the single life.

Divorce does not have to be viewed as a failure of people. It might also be viewed as a healthy growth step. Each couple knows what happened in the relationship that caused it to die. It's a two-person decision that affects many others as well. It needs sensitivity and compassion to be completed with a minimum of pain.

41

Healing Circles

My friend Hal used the term *Healing Circles* as he reflected on how many circles he had sat in during his process of recovery. In my own recovery from workaholism and caretaking, I, too, had sat in many circles where I learned to share my fears, hurts and angers. Later I shared my hopes, dreams and plans for recovery. Another close friend who is recovering from addiction tells of hundreds of healing circles he has sat in over the years that significantly changed his life.

By identifying with other people who have some of the same struggles and possibilities, we reduce our feelings of isolation and fear. It is supportive to hear stories and events so like our own and be able to listen and observe the many varied ways that people have to address and resolve problems. Emotional bonding in itself is healing.

There are healing circles for eating problems, nicotine withdrawal, drug and alcohol struggles, emotional problems, sexual problems, gambling problems, workaholism, etc.

We learn, as my friend Bedford says, "I put my hand in yours and together we can do what we cannot do alone."

This is the miracle of the healing circles.

"I put my hand in yours and together we can do what we cannot do alone." This is the miracle of the healing circles.

42

Little Bits Of Wisdom

1. Each of us will be called to account for all the good things God put on the earth which we refused to enjoy.
2. We can put on armor that will keep us from being hurt, but the same armor will hold us back and keep us from growing.
3. Wisdom is the sense of how to apply the information one has.
4. Fear is really "control madness" — the panic that sets in when one is *not* in control.
5. When going to a workshop, go as if you are a camera with a full load of film and be willing to learn and capture as much as you can. To go to a workshop with a full film defeats the purpose and you are left with nothing new.
6. By Eric Hoffer: "In times of change learners inherit the earth. And the learners find themselves perfectly equipped to deal with a world that does not exist."
7. I know I will never be as lonely in my new grief as I was in my old unhappiness.
8. People don't *CARE* how much you *KNOW* until they *KNOW* how much you *CARE*.
9. The most beautiful women in the world are wearing the courage of their convictions.

170

10. Hungry people make poor grocery shoppers — needy and lonely people make poor mates.
11. Crisis tells us it's time to change our minds and sometimes our beliefs.
12. The unwillingness to risk is what we often call security.
13. Serenity is not freedom from the storm but calm within the storm.
14. Recovery is making order out of chaos and then making changes.
15. The really happy and satisfied persons are the ones who can enjoy the scenery, even when they have to take a detour.
16. Use the talents you possess — the woods would be silent if no birds sang except the best.
17. Look for the mate who will calm the turbulence in your soul, rather than challenge it to a battle.
18. Coincidence is when God works a miracle and chooses to remain anonymous.

Part Six
More Miracles

My miracle has allowed me to develop trust in my life. It has strengthened my belief in myself and allowed me to make new choices with the confidence that all will unfold as it should. To believe in miracling is to have faith and courage to grow and change.

The following case histories are of some friends who found their miracle process in a program I facilitate called *The Reconstruction*.

Reconstruction workshops use a healing process to help participants work through the pain of being part of a dysfunctional family system. Learning, laughter, tears and sharing create a safe place to bond into a family of choice.

One entire day is a psychodrama when I guide one "star" through intense vignettes from the past. Other participants gain insight and awareness as they play roles and provide emotional feedback. Two days of experiential small-group sessions then offer each person a chance to work on personal issues.

Several of the people who agreed to share their stories have been stars. Others have been participants or small-group facilitators. Each of them has a personal miracle to share, which can provide guidance and inspiration as you follow the path of your own miracle.

My own cycle of despair and confusion was broken several years ago by my Reconstruction with Virginia Satir, author of *Peoplemaking* and an early pathfinder in the field of family therapy. One day she guided me through a tableau of events from my family's past, lovingly re-enacted by her other students. With their support, I relived my childhood and felt once again the fear and confusion of seeing my parents fight at the dinner table, of seeing my father "asleep" on the floor, of feeling my mother's love and support for me drained under the pressures of the illness of alcoholism. I re-lived my teenage and adult years through re-creation of other vignettes culled from my memory.

When the Reconstruction ended, I had re-lived a lifetime of pain. I had re-felt my feelings and discarded the ones which were no longer useful or appropriate. And I paused a moment to cherish the feelings that had given me pleasure.

I made many choices the day of my Reconstruction so that I could build from a healthy base.

43

From Shame
To Self-Worth

Paul K.

As I look back on it, I think the most powerful thing from my childhood that I brought forward in a negative way was shame. It's something my family would be horrified to think that they gave me, but they did, and I know that it comes from my father's background. He was shamed as a kid in a family with a workaholic father and a very neurotic mother, and he carried a lot of that into our relationship. It would usually come out when he was angry. He would give us one of those looks of disgust. He would discipline us and we wouldn't get loved afterwards, so my sister and I got the message, "I'm bad. I'm no good." And it carried with me so I felt insecure underneath.

There was enough strength and security in the household that it made a great conflict for me. I wasn't totally insecure. I wasn't totally secure. There was a nagging sense of nothing going right. I always blew it. I couldn't ever do it well enough. And I understood for me

177

that somehow deep inside I wasn't worth it. Even my faith that I had, a deep and living faith, didn't seem to erase all of that completely.

All this caused relationship failures, job failures, an expectation that, "somehow it was going to go wrong," and it usually did. Another part was not believing all the good things that I did do and all the skills and capabilities that I had.

I didn't even recognize that was it until I participated in the Reconstruction in October of 1986. And then the pieces began to fall together. The fact that I was sexually abused by an uncle came out and connected a whole bunch of things for me. When I did my work, which was around shame and anger, I released that back to my father and released the guilt of my favorite uncle's abuse and the sense of "my fault." I felt clean for the first time.

It was a wonderful feeling, and it lasted for a while. Then another level of healing took place at the spiritual level. It seemed to solidify what had already happened, although it was very confusing for a while. I felt so clean, then I felt so dirty again. The long-term result of it is that I'm not people-pleasing like I used to be, I'm not looking to other people to give me approval and consequently I'm getting more approval and more caring than I've ever received in my life — without having to have it.

I look at my co-dependency as looking for a relationship, a woman to make me okay. That cost me a marriage. Now I'm in a relationship where I see that I don't have to be defensive. I don't have to take everything so personally. When there is a criticism at work or when there's an issue with my wife and me, it doesn't hit me as "I'm a mistake." I made a mistake, but I'm not a mistake. While she's working through her past, as things surface in our relationship, I don't have to take it personally and be defensive. I don't have to attack her or protect myself from allowing her to be where she is. I can allow greater flexibility for myself to respond to people's needs.

Sometimes this comes up against old patterns. I would leave somebody to work it out by themselves for a while, wondering if it really means I don't care, only to find out that that is exactly what was needed. So as things don't trigger for me anymore, I find a greater freedom to be sensitive to what's going on for other people or what's going on in the situation and respond with a much wider range of choices of how to behave and act in that situation.

In my family I learned to withdraw. When there was tension and stress, I would hold back, withdraw and shut up. That's what kept me safe as a kid. But as I grew older, I would do that in relationships and work situations. Since I made a commitment to my inner child to recover, I don't have to withdraw any more. Whenever I feel like it, I can talk about it. It's safe. I choose not to withdraw from my wife. I choose to talk about what I'm feeling.

I've learned a lot in my work as a counselor because of the Reconstruction. I work with people who were in alcoholic families and who are themselves recovering from alcoholism or drug abuse. We did a lot of family-of-origin work, and it seemed like, "We can only go so far." It never really got to the deeper level. And then I rediscovered the Reconstruction work. The experiential therapy helped clean out the deeper levels of shame and guilt and anger and pain and sorrow, and that was the missing piece.

In the experiential therapy group I work with as I've gone through my own healing, my work has grown deeper and richer. I have greater freedom to not trigger my own issues, but see theirs and what we need to do. The work seems to flow, as I don't have to take so much responsibility to make something happen but can allow the flow of God's doing in people's lives. Therefore they work harder and the work that they do seems to make so much more of a difference. It's good work; it's clean; the healing comes; it triggers more things that they work on. And it's been exciting and a blessing to watch people change. I can see them get better, have more freedom in their lives, more freedom to be there for other people in appropriate and healthy ways. That's been a joy, and I am thankful.

44

My Needs Count.
I Have Rights.

Ed W.

It used to be awful. Frightening. Lonely. Angry. Anxious. All the time. What will happen if she finds out how crazy I am? Why can't I be satisfied with myself? With anything? With anyone?

At least the last four generations on both sides of my family suffered from repression (religious), compulsion, addiction and mental illness. My parents were respectable middle-class alcoholics, obsessed with appearances, who gave their three sons (I was the oldest) everything money could buy: summer camps, tutors, psychiatrists, piano lessons, pool and ping pong tables. They gave little or nothing of themselves, except constant criticism and verbal and physical abuse. They bickered or argued daily. I spent a lot of time protecting my mother and little brothers from my father's abusive rages. No one protected me. I loved it when my cousins or other company came to visit because it seemed safe then. Otherwise it was usually scary around our house.

My dad had had polio and walked with a limp. We used to play outside, in the attic or down in the basement — places he was unlikely to come or would be slow getting there. He was a person to be avoided. We spent time with my parents doing what they, not we, enjoyed doing: going to concerts with my mom; working out at the YMCA with my dad, the former athlete/coach. We couldn't wear what we liked. Forced haircuts were a bi-weekly ordeal. Shopping for shoes (or anything else) meant certain conflict and abuse.

At times, from age 13 to 40 (when I finally entered recovery), I ate and worked compulsively, was a juvenile kleptomaniac, a compulsive gambler and addicted to alcohol, exercise, sex and various drugs (particularly nicotine and marijuana). Although a star college gymnast and an honor student in law school, I never felt successful, despite rapid career advancement and acclaim. My failed co-dependent first marriage (eight years), although riddled with heartache and affairs, nevertheless produced two wonderful children. I raised my daughter with my ACoA/workaholic second wife (eleven years). Our household and marriage always looked good on the outside, but I was always plagued by compulsion, fear and self-doubt within. Drug- and alcohol-related health problems cropped up periodically. I seemed either super-responsible or super-irresponsible about everything and everyone, rarely able to focus on myself and my real needs.

Teenager/parent conflicts with my daughter led me to a family therapist, who finally diagnosed my main problem: ACoA. Attending a Reconstruction workshop in the fall of 1985 and the Caron Foundation's five-day program in the spring of 1986 increased my self-awareness and got me honest, clean and sober, but my chronic low self-worth and many compulsions persisted. I started going to AA, Al-Anon and other 12-step meetings. I had sobriety without serenity. Finally I decided I needed to be the star of my own Reconstruction.

What I Learned From My Reconstruction

I learned self-respect during my Reconstruction by remembering, re-living and finally understanding a little boy's nightmare. My nightmare: the fear, the screaming, the constant abuse. I was so brave, trying as best as I could to protect my little brothers and myself, trying to help my helpless mom, fighting my drunken "crazy" father.

"I'm not an animal! I'm a person!" I finally felt that. I finally meant that. I mattered. I meant something to myself. I began to care about myself deeply for reasons I could finally feel and understand. For once, I could see how powerless I was as a child (and in many ways still am). I was trapped. I felt alone and threatened. But I did the best I could and I survived.

I'd been so angry at my father for so long. I never realized how ignored I felt, how much I was hurt by my mother. My mother who stayed with him. My mother who rarely nurtured me but who did the best she could, who had little sensitivity and few skills for parenting. She was a sick pup all her life, concealing self-doubt behind a mask of sophistication. A high-class suburban drunk, incapacitated by migraine headaches. I could never understand why she didn't take us and leave my father. During my Reconstruction I realized that she couldn't. She didn't feel she could survive on her own.

I realized how I short-circuited emotionally about age 12. I overloaded with fear, anger and self-doubt, and shut down in silent pain. I remembered and felt anew what it was like. I finally understood why I'd medicated my pain for 30 years with gambling, food, sex, alcohol, work and drugs. I finally found the other me deep down inside myself, in hiding all those years: sweet, tender, funny, hopeful and smart. I felt how tired I was of playing the hero, faking my way through life with secret fears.

I could see and feel for the first time how sick and limited my parents were. They couldn't love us because they didn't know how. My reactions to my childhood were not my fault and were finally understandable and acceptable to me. What a miracle I survived! I can accept and live with my lifelong pain as it finally diminishes.

And my shame evaporated as I came to understand the clear connection between childhood sexual abuse by my grandmother and sexual addiction throughout my adult life. I learned about boundaries. And I learned about time. The scary part of my life was over. I was choosing a time of peace.

How It Is Now

Now I'm calm a lot of the time. It's better. I'm better. I am. I don't have parenting parents so I parent myself. My marriage is innominate.

At times I am my own spouse and companion. I am truly lovable and capable. I am a constant recovering person, grateful and patient. I don't need to even love my new 12-step way of life: AA, NA, Al-Anon, and SAA (Sex Addicts Anonymous).

My old marriage is over, but it may be re-born if my wife, who has entered recovery, progresses. I am able to be intimate now. I am often very lonely, cut off from family and former friends. My parents' active addictions make relations with them difficult. I avoid seeing them too often to avoid the pain. My alcoholic mother is dying from cancer. My cross-addicted father is killing himself but can't see it as I now can. God is letting me accept the things I cannot change, but I do not feel serene.

I feel better about myself. I am a cool neat person. I'm addicted. I need a lot of help and I'm not afraid to ask for it. I'm strong enough and smart enough to accept the help I desperately need.

I'm on the move, changing, my values shifting. Somehow my lifelong craving for wealth, status and power diminishes as my self-love grows. I am making new friends in recovery. For the first time since puberty I have some real male friends. I no longer masturbate or need sex every day. I have self-confidence and renewed interest in my work, which I no longer fear. Business stress is tiring but not frightening.

I now know that pain, which I can cope with, is a normal part of my otherwise joyous life.

My needs count. I have rights.

I am a child of God. My life is now becoming a prayer that is its own answer.

45

How It Used To Be

Joan M.

I felt inadequate intellectually so I married a super-intellectual man and set myself up to be critical, harsh and judgmental of myself. I felt inadequate as a female and was mesmerized by a man who said I had a beautiful body, and allowed myself to be victimized.

When my first marriage of 18 years ended, I never dealt with my loss of roles as wife, mother and caretaker. Instead I found a man whose childhood had been devastating and centered my life on his well-being, teaching him to deal with his own pain, loneliness and inadequacies, and getting my good feelings of self from his progress. I didn't know how to have a relationship with my children without being resentful, interfering and destructive, so I removed myself entirely from them and missed out on a good part of their lives.

I never learned how to get my needs met as a child; therefore, I never learned how to get my needs met as an adult. I was incredibly serious, lonely, angry, empty. I was isolated . . . my magical thinking wasn't working . . . time was not healing the wounds.

At work I am a valuable employee and with each proficiency rating the message of generations is, "Work harder and do more." One year

I received a proficiency rating that was excellent. However, it was rated five points lower than the previous year, and I was devastated.

I was bankrupt emotionally, physically and spiritually. Everything I was trying was not working. My body began to deteriorate. I felt like I was dying, and I didn't know how to stop the process. I trusted unwisely and endured a great deal of disappointment and felt victimized. I didn't know how to say no, so I set myself up to be taken advantage of repeatedly. At this time the inner child did not exist in me. My new life had more quality, but not for me . . . I didn't know why. I knew that to do for others, was to be me. I was lonely and tired and didn't want to do for others anymore. For me not to do for others was to die.

What I Learned From My Reconstruction

I learned that without a support system I won't make it. I learned that I can have a healthy relationship with my children. I don't have to beg for crumbs to exist. I learned that the child within me is alive and well, and I can protect and care for her. I learned that I am worthwhile and loving, that I can select caring people with wisdom, that I have the tools to overcome my disease. I learned I am capable of confronting the monsters of yesterday and killing them and going on. I learned that I am loved and have value. That I have an opportunity for new beginnings. I learned to forgive myself, accept my disease and go on and feel the feelings of pain, loneliness and despair.

I could do that because I had a network of people who loved me when I wasn't lovable, who understood me before I understood myself and who always allowed me to be who I was when I was.

How It Is Now

In my recovery I can see more clearly what I am responsible for: me, in work and in relationships. Little sayings will creep into my awareness, like "Mind your own business," "That's not your job, Joan," "What other people think of you is none of your business," "Hang loose," "Keep it simple," "Let go."

I don't go to empty wells for water. I keep connected to people who care about me, who know my weaknesses and invite me to grow. In recovery I see brilliant colors. My spirituality is centered. I find peace and joy in quietness. I do things for me without guilt. As long as I listen to my feelings, honor them and deal with them, I stay out of my illness. In my recovery I have many intimate relationships. I listen to the dreams and fantasies of the child who never had a chance to speak them before.

I follow the extremes from the disbelief to the absurd and know that when I need it, reality steps in and I am okay. I rejoice in the sanity of my recovery, and I continue my journey.

Because my support system has meant so much to me, I want to share two letters I received after my Reconstruction from group members.

From Garth, Who Played My Youngest Son, Warren.

I've thought quite a bit about the events and the way they affected me. The amazing aspect of my playing Warren was how well it relates to my life. I feel as if my mother left me when I was 10 or 11 and I still have not forgiven her. I resent her, actually, and I can't be near her without feeling terribly uneasy. I'm even getting angry as I sit here and write.

The fact that my mother gave me notice that she wanted a real relationship with me didn't mean I was willing to try and return the effort, because I haven't. This is very difficult for me to write, and I want to stop, but I won't. Ideally, I would simply have a good relationship with Mom, but there is something that is blocking that, and that something is the work I need to get through so that I can stop seeing my mother through tainted eyes.

I saw a real sincere need for reconciliation on your part with Warren, and the most important thing I can say is don't be surprised if Warren has some anger or resentment. All you can do is let him know you are there for him, and then he has the option of taking you up on the offer or not. It might be that your invitation to him may act as an incentive for him to try to work through some issues with you. I hope everything works out, and I hope this will help you. Thank you for giving me the opportunity that you have, and may God be with you.

From Ruth, A Member Of The Group At The Reconstruction.

Your work with Garth as the son you feared you had lost moved me deeply. I felt you showed great courage in working through that particularly. To reveal your deepest relationships — things you had done that you had suffered over — not just once but again and again that day, showed great trust in Sharon, in yourself and the process.

I thought, "How wonderful to be able to do that!" It was the ability to go with your feelings around one event and then move to another that I learned from the rage, tears, rejection, shame, the whole gamut. That was a strengthening gift from you. It was incredible.

The other most impressive part of your Reconstruction was the decision-making process in the conclusion. Listening to you making choices and your sharing how much distance, how much reconciliation you would be working on, hearing your real choices made on the basis of both feeling and reality, inspired me to look differently and searchingly at my own circle of family and friends. I feel much freer to dilute and diminish some marginal relationships. This from me, who is known to be a friend for life, for better or worse. I feel enriched and strengthened, as well as having a sense of the waste of how I have carried people along at my own expense. It was important to see it done. I don't think there was a parent or a counselor among us who wouldn't want to have their kids or clients have the opportunity you are offering your children.

46

Feel — Deal — Heal

Mary R.

ᐯ "Always a bridesmaid; never a bride" aptly describes my experience as a Reconstruction addict. After participating in 25 Reconstruction weeks since 1981, I feel reconstructed by osmosis, although I have never been a star. And perhaps that is a statement about my own slow recovery from co-dependency.

When I first heard about Sharon, I was completing a Masters Degree, specializing in marriage and family issues around addictive behaviors. I had been in recovery from chemical dependency for 13 years, and my husband and six grown children had supported my efforts to complete my education after the nest emptied. I was trying my wings as one of the early members of liberated womanhood, scared one minute and thrilled the next, as I began to discover I really did have an identity separate from my many roles. I struggled through pangs of guilt as I broke years of rules about women's roles and the myth of finding happiness and fulfillment through filling others' needs.

In 1979 as I completed my undergraduate work, the first rumblings about family treatment were being heard and I became curious —

motivated out of my own experience as a recovering person, daughter, wife, mother, sister. There had not been alcoholism in my family of origin, and I saw my own addiction as the result of stress and old guilts that had found immediate relief from chemicals when I was 30 years old.

With this background I traveled to Minneapolis for my first Reconstruction in 1981. By then I had read Sharon's pamphlets and had heard her speak at two or three workshops. I could not get enough. I felt a soul response to her message and knew I must learn more from her.

I had no idea what to expect at a Reconstruction. I went to learn more, to train with Sharon. I remember "observing" all week, truly believing, "I'm fine, thank you." As I look back now, I feel great compassion for that therapist that was me. I was working as director of a five-day family program, not realizing how much all those families were teaching me. Sharon's work was the glue that began putting so many pieces together.

I began to schedule more weeks with Sharon every chance I could get. I saw them as my treatment as well as my training. I knew that I needed to remain clear and clean with my own family-of-origin work in order to be effective with my clients. I never even considered being a "star," there was so little left or known about my family. I saw no major areas of concern in my life. After a very rocky first 10 years of sobriety, my recovery was progressing beautifully, and I even experienced that elusive goal called serenity on occasion.

I began to research family treatment programs around the country (using all of them as my own treatment as well as training). Because of what I learned, I began truly dealing with unfinished issues from my childhood. The term "co-dependency" was still unknown, but I began to see my hero personality had developed from the same kind of family system as those where there had been alcoholism. My delusion began to lift. Each time I shared the experience of a Reconstruction, I identified and began to share more and more with Sharon and my peers. In the meantime, when Sharon moved, I followed — to Texas, California and South Dakota. I have been a member of the group leader staff since 1982 and they have become the nucleus of my family of choice, an ever-widening network of friends throughout the world with whom I can share that instant intimacy that results from being able to dispense with old defensive facades and roles. I have whittled away at those defenses and discovered a sensitive little girl named Mary Helen, who had to give up her childhood at 5½ years. She and I are friends today and celebrate our ability to feel our feelings and be congruent.

In addition to my own healing, I had to learn I cannot "fix" anyone else. It was a struggle, but I did start learning how to truly let go and let God. As miracles do happen when I get out of the way, many of my family members are also finding their paths to recovery through Reconstruction and treatment for co-dependency. After 36 years of marriage, my husband and I are happier than we have ever been.

Now as I celebrate my first 20 years of recovery, I reflect on the "angels" who have guided me out of the darkness. I see Sharon and her Reconstruction process as that inspiration the past seven years.

I am reminded of a favorite past-time of mine — jigsaw puzzles. A box of 1000 pieces spread out on a table finds no meaning until I can match the straight edges and at least establish an outline. I see my 12-step program as having provided that function as I tried to pick up the pieces of my life 20 years ago. I made headway in the various sections of the puzzle — finding the sky, forests and castles — but the Reconstruction process has shown me how to put all those segments together so I can see the bigger picture. I owe Sharon and all the stars and members of "the family" a debt of love and thanks for helping me find the beauty in my puzzle picture. Because of this kind of treatment — going through the pain rather than controlling or avoiding it — a tremendous joy and true serenity is possible. It is my hope that there will someday be a new slogan added to those like "One day at a time" and "First things first." The new one will read: "Feel — Deal — Heal!"

47

From Frozen To Feeling

Cheryl K.

How it used to be? Trapped. Unable to express my feelings, living in fear that someone would find out who the real me was and when they did, they wouldn't like me. I came from a quiet low energy family. So consequently I looked for excitement and lived in a fantasy world much of the time. Anger was not acceptable in my family so I never learned how to resolve conflicts. What I did learn was how to stuff the feeling and get quiet. Working hard was the way to get attention. I was a mascot who wanted to be a hero. Heroes were perfect. So I performed. I felt like I was on stage most of my life, trying to get a perfect 10.

I depended on others for my self-esteem — their approval could make or break me. My self-worth depended on what I had around me. I know today that the child within me was very needy but I didn't know how to nurture her. I attempted to get my needs met through people and things. Somewhere around age 16 I lost my spiritual connection. Over the next 20 years I felt God had deserted me.

In my adult life I became a professional caretaker. By the age of 18 I discovered that cigarettes helped keep my feelings down. I felt powerful and in control when I smoked. I had found something that would help me feel better. But inwardly I felt like a fake. In order to make that feeling go away I smoked more, tried harder, worked longer hours, got more education, married someone safe. More, more, more, I needed more. Something within me was crying out for the love that I didn't get at work or at home. So I looked elsewhere — an affair. My world began to crumble. I felt ashamed and guilty about having an affair, but was unwilling to end it. So I got divorced.

This relationship was never quiet or dull. I knew that this man needed me, and I was willing to take whatever was dished out with no complaints. I had no boundaries. I felt so badly about myself that I would allow myself to be put in dangerous situations where I was physically abused and came back for more.

There's that word again — more.

I married that man because somehow I knew I needed him a lot more than he needed me. Together we got sicker and sicker. To my surprise I found out he was chemically dependent. I became obsessed with the need to fix him.

In 1981 I got into recovery from co-dependency through going to Al-Anon meetings. Gradually I began to find my spiritual connection through working the 12-step program. About one year into the program I felt stuck. The program wasn't working the way it did in the beginning. I decided I needed something more so I attended a Reconstruction workshop. There my feelings began to unthaw. My body reacted severely to this. I sneezed and my eyes watered all week. The predominant feeling I experienced that week was rage. What a day when I let some of it out! I didn't die and people still liked me.

My therapy became Reconstruction workshops. I went every four to six months for two years. I worked on an issue, then went home to integrate it into my life. I found out over the next two years that I was a rageful woman, a hurting woman, a needy woman and a strong loving woman. It took all of those workshops for me to trust enough to be able to surrender to the Reconstruction process myself.

I had the privilege of being asked by my husband to be at his Reconstruction in September of 1984. It was at his Reconstruction that Sharon encouraged me to be reconstructed. I agreed to have the process done.

Over the next year I gathered information from my family of origin. I was fearful to approach my family with questions because our family "doesn't shake their dirty linen in public." Later I felt love and caring as each of my family members gave me their individual time and shared with me their perceptions of our life together. And our perceptions of our early lives together were all very different.

My Reconstruction was in September of 1985. When I reflect back to the day, my eyes fill with tears of joy. It was the culmination of 2½ years of putting the pieces of my life together. It was a day of clarity, setting boundaries, taking my freedom from the disease and reclaiming my personal power. My eyes were opened. I truly opened my heart and embraced my child within. She is enough!!

The day of my Reconstruction was also a spiritual happening. For me to trust Sharon and the process was a spiritual experience. To surrender to reality was a spiritual experience. I also learned that by sharing all my feelings, I set boundaries. Boundaries give me freedom. Freedom gives me choices.

Today I know I always have choices. I have learned to negotiate and set boundaries. Conflict resolution is attainable. Solutions come from many sources.

Since my Reconstruction, I feel my spiritual connection growing and strengthening. Life goes on with its ups and downs, but my connection to my Higher Power and inner child has helped me through those times. The intimacy I now experience with my mate is a connection of the soul. I take care of myself physically, emotionally and spiritually. I am reaching out to people when I need help. The relationship with one of my stepsons is improving constantly. I accept my parents with a knowledge that they did the best they knew how. I have established a family of choice where I can share intimate feelings and life experiences. My recovery keeps changing and I resist less. That's progress.

48

A New Lease On Life

Jim K.

I have found it difficult to put in words, on paper, what my Reconstruction has meant to me. I can engage in long periods of sharing the recovery process with others, and as I talk, a deeper meaning of the Reconstruction process always becomes evident to me. As the time lengthens since the actual event took place, its importance has become more and more evident.

In September 1981, I began recovery from the disease of alcoholism. In the next year I did everything I was told I should do — six AA meetings a week, professional support groups, pray and meditate twice a day, talk to my sponsor regularly, read the "Big Book" over and over.

In September 1982, I was ready to commit suicide. My physical health was returning. I had a good job, professional and personal respect and an improving relationship with my wife. And I wanted to die. I was filled with anger and grief and didn't know what to do with these strange feelings which I had never allowed myself to experience before. More meetings, more prayer, more reading just didn't help. At the age of 49 I had to accept that intellect and reason couldn't resolve all life's problems. I knew then that my spiritual being must connect to my Higher Power on a feeling level.

Fortunately for me, one of my sponsors directed me to Adult Children of Alcoholics meetings. Unfortunately this same person relapsed after over eight years of abstinence. He was deeply in need of rigid control of his entire personal and professional environment. I realize now that that was exactly the way I was prior to beginning the Reconstruction process. Today I can truly say that I am in recovery, not just abstinent.

For me the process began when I attended my first Reconstruction program — two years before the date of my own Reconstruction. I needed to develop trust, to feel love and caring, to be accepted and primarily to be validated. Had I never felt all of this, I would never have been willing to have my own Reconstruction done.

In my first workshop I was able to play the role of a minister, who was a kind nurturing person. This helped to open up my eyes, to break through my prejudices concerning religion/spirituality (at that time I didn't know there was any difference). I always felt that I had come from a long line of "drunks," in the most derogatory sense of the word. But I learned as I traced my own family tree that I came from a long line of ministers, ending three generations before mine. So I came full circle.

Later in a workshop I had a major myth exploded. I hid behind a false guilt and major grandiosity concerning responsibility for my mother's death. One of the group leaders then, who I choose to call Joe for lack of a better name, directly confronted me about my defenses. I needed this for it was the last wall, the biggest barrier that I used to separate me from a true surrender. I made a firm conscious decision then that I wanted to go through the Reconstruction process.

As part of preparation for the Reconstruction I was forced to go back to visit living family members. From this I gained tremendous insights into the dynamics of my family and some basic facts became evident. I gained understanding of the lives of my parents and why they chose to live their lives as they had. I came to realize that my brother and two sisters and I had entirely different perceptions of our family as we were growing. I know today that we all four lived entirely different lives although we lived together; our relations with our parents were entirely different.

On the day of my Reconstruction I felt a total trust in Sharon and the Reconstruction process. I had no need for defenses. I felt a total communion with the God of my understanding. It was the first day of my life when I felt no fear, and I was amply rewarded.

On the day after my Reconstruction I felt a total mental emptiness. I was perceptive, receptive, willing and eager to go on. Most of all I knew I had a new family — the Reconstruction community. I was no longer willing to hold on to myths, empty promises and unfounded hope. I knew where I could always go for nurturing and love.

My life has continued to improve, in fact, it improves as much as I allow it. I experience uncomfortable and even intensely painful times but I always come through stronger on the other side. I experience feelings which used to be only words, but none of them have killed me. I know today that the only limits on possibilities in my life are those which are self-imposed. I have a continually improving communion with my God and I'm able to lay out all the bad beside the gratitude for all the good. I have a newer, deeper understanding of myself and I can speak about my positive attributes without diminishing them.

And finally — intimacy. Each day I gain a newer, deeper knowing of what intimacy with myself means. Because of this I have a wonderful relationship with my wife, which continues to improve daily. I am healthy, physically and mentally. I have a job I enjoy, and I experience a seemingly limitless number of choices in all aspects of my life.

I know that I will never be able to fully comprehend what the Reconstruction process has meant to me because it continues to change daily. It is the absolute cornerstone of the foundation of my life and recovery.

My natural birthday is September 15. My AA birthday is September 21. My Reconstruction birthday is September 18. Only God could have planned that.

49

From Pain To Choice

Judy P.

V My father was very angry and very abusive most of his life. He didn't drink — neither one of my parents drank — so I couldn't understand why he was always so angry. I felt like I must have done something wrong but I didn't know what.

He constantly told me I was a "no-good bitch," so I did a lot of things throughout my life to live up to his expectations.

I was sexually abused by a neighbor as a child, raped at age 17, was on diet pills from age 10 until 25. I married right out of high school and ended up with the same type of abusive man my father was. We had a son, I decided I had to get out and I got a divorce. I went to school and became a nurse so I could support myself and my son. My second marriage was to a man who wanted to take care of me, who was so good to me I couldn't stand it. That also ended in divorce.

After other abusive relationships, periods of deep depression and feeling so worthless and no good I wanted to die, I met another man. When we met, he had been single for a little over three months. His wife had committed suicide. We both were very needy and met and fell in love immediately. We were married three months later and thought we would live happily ever after. He had four sons, two dogs, and I had one son, one dog. We combined them to make the Brady Bunch.

However, there was a lot of turmoil in all of our lives and the blending of the two families was not exactly like the Brady Bunch. We had a lot of ups and downs in our relationship, a lot of problems with our children and even the dogs.

In this marriage my husband gained 100 pounds and I gained 100 pounds in approximately five and a half years. We both were under a lot of stress. At the beginning of the marriage I drank quite a bit of wine and would medicate with gin and a few other things. I took some anti-depressants and tranquilizers, anything to try and calm myself down and to live in this environment. I had made up my mind that I was not going to leave this relationship, but it wasn't very long before I decided that again I wanted to run, I wanted to get out, I wanted someone to love me and I didn't feel that my needs were getting met here.

My husband was never abusive to me physically, but I realize now he was verbally abusive, telling me I was unacceptable and wasn't doing things right. When he would say I was unacceptable, I would translate it to the script that I had grown up with — that I was a no-good bitch. Even though he didn't say it that way, that was what I heard.

My husband was a physician, and in the beginning of the marriage I got a lot of self-esteem out of being a physician's wife. I thought I'll show you people I am something, I am somebody. Then my whole self-image just started going downhill. I began gaining weight and looked worse and worse. I was not the mother I would have liked to be, to my son and my step-sons. I just found myself barely functioning. It was all I could do to get through the day. I had made up my mind that I was not going to get divorced again, that I had already been divorced twice and the only way I saw out of this relationship was death. And so I tried to get up enough nerve to commit suicide but I just couldn't bring myself to it.

One evening an incident happened with my biological son and I felt like my husband would be in a rage when he came home and I was scared. I didn't know what to do, so I started drinking. I decided I wanted to die in a blackout, and I took an overdose.

It was at that time or the next day I knew that I was very, very ill and needed help. I called a counselor, who said I needed to go into a psychiatric hospital and would probably be there a minimum of three to six months. At that time I didn't really care. It was okay, I just wanted somebody to do something with me. But my husband wasn't too thrilled about me being away for that period of time or going into a psychiatric hospital because people end up in there, in and out, in and out, in and out.

I had talked to a friend, who talked with another physician who was in recovery and said he knew just the place for me to go. And that place was to a Reconstruction workshop in Rapid City, South Dakota. Well, it sounded real crazy to me, real bizarre. But he said, "Just trust me. I believe that you'll get a lot more out there in a week than you'll get in three months in a mental hospital."

So I figured what did I have to lose, and I tried it.

And I believe it was the beginning, the rebirth of my life.

A lot of things happened for me out in Rapid City. It was a very special place to me. It's where the spiritual part of me became alive again. I believed I was dead emotionally and spiritually. All I kept thinking was, I wanted to die.

But things started happening for me. I got in touch with all the abuse that I'd received as a child, the sexual abuse of being raped as a teenager and all the shame and guilt that I had carried with me all these years, how bad I felt about myself. Here I was able to talk about it, do some anger work and be accepted. The greatest thing that happened was being accepted by all these people, even though I had told them all these horrible things that had happened to me. And I believe that's when the spiritual part of the program started for me.

I found myself in the chapel down on my knees, praying for God to take these feelings away from me and to help me. This was when my life began.

I left that Reconstruction feeling very high and good about myself. However, after I was home maybe a couple of weeks, I began to have some of the same old feelings creep back in. At that time I didn't understand a whole lot about what a 12-step program was, but I started going to some meetings, and I found myself three months later back out to a Reconstruction. I did another piece of work on some more things that had happened in my life.

I went back home and started working on my own program, but I was unhappy because my husband wasn't doing the same thing. People kept telling me, you need to just take care of yourself, it's your program, it's not his program. I had a hard time with that, and they kept saying the only person you can change is yourself. And I was very resentful of that at first because if he would only change, I would be okay.

As I began to work the program and turn things over, my life did start changing. I went back in July to another Reconstruction. At that time I decided I wanted to do this process myself, that this was something I needed.

So I began to get all the information together about my childhood, hunting up records on my grandparents and just looking at records and I found a lot of information that began to give me healing.

A big thing I got in touch with was all the abuse that my parents had suffered. They both had been severely abused children. They were raised in orphanages, and my father was severely abused for all of his acting out. My mother also was ridiculed and abused because she didn't know who her father was.

What I later found out was that I had picked up all their shame. I had carried a lot of their pain and their anger and acted it out myself. I didn't know where a lot of those feelings came from, but that was one of the big pieces I got out of my Reconstruction.

I had also done the same thing in this marriage. My husband never had to get angry because I carried the anger for both of us and then I would proceed to act it out. I didn't want to look at what was going on inside of me because if I stopped blaming everyone else, I had to take responsibility for me.

I was reconstructed in January of 1986. It was probably one of the longest, most painful, most happy, most healing days of my entire life. A lot of things became evident to me: that I had been a victim in my life and I had continued to set myself up to be a victim.

I had been abused by men all my life, managing to pick up where they left off and find abusive relationships to get into. I even picked a religion at one time that was male-oriented and the females were nothing. Even the profession I chose, nursing, is a job where you're subservient to the male, even choosing the operating room which is particularly male-dominated. I had just lived this role out — victim, victim, victim, poor me, poor me, all the while feeling bad, hating people, angry, lashing out and never understanding why, never knowing where all this came from.

I was only able to see this pattern through the Reconstruction process. Sharon has such a loving way of putting it in front of you that you can't help but see it. I think, however, the biggest gift I got out of my Reconstruction was love and acceptance. I had my whole life in going through this process in front of 50 people. I was accepted and loved by every one of them, and through that love and acceptance I was able to start loving and accepting me. I started to believe that I was a child of God and that He loved me for me. And I was able to start loving me then. I was able to see how I had got myself into a lot of the situations because I just wanted to be loved.

The biggest thing was that I found myself and I found little Judy and I've been able to love and nurture her. There are days that I still put her on hold and forget about her, but most of the time I take care of myself. I still have trouble at times, I get into the victim role but I don't stay there as long as I used to. When I feel the pain and when I know there's pain and when I have a lot of unsettledness, I know I have to stop and look at my life and ask what's happening, how have I set this up, how have I caused this? But I can't even put into words how much relief I've had in my life since my Reconstruction.

All night long after my Reconstruction, I replayed it over and over and over. One of the things that became very evident to me was that each time I had got myself into some type of trouble, alcohol or pills were around it. So the next day I had to look at whether I was an alcoholic. And that's when I began my recovery for alcoholism.

I've become very involved in the AA program, working the 12-step program with that, OA and adult children issues. Lots of good things have happened for me in recovery. I lost 65 pounds after I did my Reconstruction. I was able to get in touch with all the rage and anger that I had saved up for years being such a victim. As I was able to let go of all the pain in my past, I didn't have the urge to eat as much. However, as I lost some weight very rapidly, I knew that I did have to go on the OA plan because I do believe that food is an addiction and when I eat sugar, I do set myself up to binge.

After my Reconstruction, my life really started changing because I started changing.

Some time after my Reconstruction, my husband went to treatment for his eating disorder. After a difficult time we both were able to surrender to the process of recovery and choose to give up controlling each other.

And so our coupleship has begun. It was like a whole new rebirth
for both of us. We've been at this now for six months, he working his
program and I working mine. Many days it's real hard for me to stay
out of his program. I know some days it's real hard for him to stay out
of mine. But what we both know is that I have to work this program
for me and he has to work this program for him. We need to stand
alone, and when we're able to stand alone, we're able to stand
together. One of the biggest beauties of my recovery is being able to
have a relationship with someone who I truly love and being able to
say what I need to say to him and he being able to say what he needs
to say to me.

Another big reward has been watching the children get into their
own recovery programs. Four out of five of our children have had at
least one week of co-dependency therapy. One of our sons is active
in AA, he's working his program and the other son has been through
treatment for co-dependency. So I've had just reward after reward in
watching them develop and grow. They're doing what they need to
do to take care of themselves. They're making a lot of progress, much
further than I ever could have hoped to have been at that age. They
have awareness that I never had at their age.

Many days it's difficult. Many days I still find myself in the same old
pitfalls, but my life is so much better. I don't feel like I have to go out
and kill myself, I don't feel like I need to die. It's just so different
living a life thinking that you're worthwhile, that you are somebody
and that what you have to say counts.

At this time I am working as a drug and alcohol therapist and co-
dependent therapist. I'm an inpatient primary counselor. I also have
had the honor of working for Sharon at Reconstructions and being a
group leader. I love going to South Dakota because it's where my
spiritual part begins, where my recovery began. Each time I go to the
Black Hills, I get a breath of fresh renewal, and it reminds me of
where I came from and how far I've come.

I also have a renewed relationship with my parents, one that I've
never had before. After I was able to see what their lives had been
like, what they had gone through, I was able to forgive. I was angry
about what had happened, and I had to go through a lot of pain and
anger, but then I was able to come to the acceptance part, to forgive
and to let go. It's really neat to be able to talk to them as adults, to
give my parents hugs — something that I never did before. And they

give me hugs back. They try to understand my program and ask little questions, and there are many days I want to say, "You need to go and do this and this," but I know that it'll be in God's time.

I have so many rewards in my recovery for me and also watching my children and husband choose their own recovery programs.

I am eternally grateful.

50

I Am Worth Recovery

Kathryn C.

On the surface my physician husband and I exemplified the American Dream. We were well educated and affluent with four wonderful children between us. Underneath the facade and beautiful trappings, however, the American Dream was a nightmare of disease and destruction from addiction and co-dependency.

I believed my husband had a problem with alcohol. The fact that I was an emotional mess never entered my mind. If HE would stop drinking, then the lonely weekends and holidays would be good again. Drunken slobbery rapings would cease. The constant fear of beatings would end. The children could have friends over and we could entertain without fear of embarrassment or incident. The unbelievable stories to cover accidents/poor behavior would be no more. The terrifying rides with a severely inebriated driver would be no more. Then we would all live happily ever after.

I had labored hard up to that point in our lives to make all of the above dreams come true. Like other co-dependents I had spent years bending, flexing, changing, fixing, manipulating, doing the impossible to the point of totally losing my own identity.

After years of prayer, counseling, a period of sobriety for my husband followed by relapse, I found myself in an Al-Anon meeting feeling totally defeated.

At the first meeting, much to my surprise, I felt love, true acceptance and understanding. It was as if they had known me all of my life. After talking with a therapist for the first time, I accepted the fact that I was sick, too, and needed help. Two things she said struck and have stuck with me over the years.

1. I could divorce my husband, be free of fear and begin to enjoy my life again. BUT if I did not treat my disease of co-alcoholism (known today as co-dependency) I was guaranteed to attach myself to another man who was just as sick if not worse than my current husband.
2. Recovery from this disease is very painful. In order to find myself and gain serenity I must be willing to experience that pain to get on the other side of it.

I separated from my husband for a time, but returned home and began counseling with him as part of his treatment for alcoholism. Through this, I learned about the 12 steps of recovery.

By working my steps, the painful honesty of dealing with an affair triggered my memory of six years of incest as a child. *Big-time pain!* So painful I ceased to function. It was necessary to acquire a therapist outside the group to help me work through and come out on the other side of that pain. In doing so, we discovered that the core of my disease was Multiple Personality Disorder. My God, how could that be possible? Only "crazy" people have that!

What a jolt! I had just made peace with myself for the 27 years of blocking the incestual happenings, which brought on all manner of self-destructive behavior. Now this. How much more of my life did I wipe out? How many more painful realizations must I now face? Whatever happened to "If only my husband would quit drinking, we could live happily ever after?"

Right then and there I became an ardent believer that sometimes the family members are sicker than the alcoholic. And that living with the alcoholic did not make me sick. I was sick long before I ever met him.

I was the first split personality my therapist had counseled. He suggested I make peace with my parts. That plus work with two AA members helped me to integrate about six weeks after the diagnosis was made. At long last I found the real me.

Integration was great! Each of my four personalities was able to share when she had begun. I had not been aware of my blackout periods until then. My sudden failing grades in my last two years of high school finally made sense. One personality would be in class, one would do the homework and another would take the exam. It explained my almost autistic characteristics as a child. I came to the embarrassing realization that the accusations of my sexual activities in my college years were true. I could finally understand why I had such difficulty losing weight on a diet — only ONE of me went on a diet.

Surprisingly, as more and more truth about myself came to the surface, the happier and more peaceful I became. The four of us were in agreement most of the time. If not, we would discuss the situation among ourselves and come up with a workable solution.

One of my fellow Al-Anoners once commented, "You know, you have your own Al-Anon group meeting wherever you go." That certainly was true, and what a comfort to me. With integration I was able to recapture most of the blackout ties. I was also able to see the continual subconscious battles for control that had gone on for who knows how long. After all the painful work before integration, the following 14 months of peace and compatibility were welcomed indeed.

Meanwhile my husband and I were still struggling to make our marriage work. My therapist asked that we answer a number of questions that would divulge our basic characteristics. I asked to have four answer sheets. Each of my known personalities answered the questions accordingly. The results showed four completely different people. Only one had the characteristics to be truly compatible with my husband. Unfortunately she was not the real me.

All four of us decided that each one would do their own fourth and fifth steps. That way each one of us would be free of the wreckage of the past. Another awareness was of four different handwritings, along with the realization that only one of us married and/or liked being with my husband. But I was happy to be at peace within, my husband was sober and we were in agreement on the 12-step programs. Life was grand. I didn't want to look at the facts.

Then blackouts! For the first time I became consciously aware that they were happening. Then two more unknown personalities surfaced. I became painfully aware of just how ugly Multiple Personality Disorder truly is. Hopelessness set in. I became suicidal. My therapist said I wouldn't gain anything by doing that. I said, "Oh, yes I will. At least all six will be dead and there will never be seven or eight."

Before taking that drastic step, I took time to prioritize my obligations. All were accomplished except the last two. Ironically, the first of the two was the annual four-day Medical Symposium on Alcoholism directed by Dr. Joseph Cruse at the Eisenhower Medical Center in Rancho Mirage. That year Sharon Wegscheider-Cruse spoke on the disease of co-dependency and Patsy Crandall gave an overview of the Reconstruction process. I was so impressed with the idea I gave Sharon a check to reserve a space for me, with the thought that if I lived long enough, I believed it would help to make me one person as God had intended.

Two days later I fulfilled my last obligation, which was to be a worker at an Oral Roberts healing. After all of the prayers for specific illnesses were complete, Oral and Richard asked, "Do any of you suffer from 'any kind' of DIS-EASE?" I could certainly say "amen" to that. I privately joined in with the prayers of Oral, Richard and thousands of others in support of my very desperate petition to God. I couldn't believe it! Could it be that easy? I was whole!!!!! No more voices — no more parts — just Kathryn. Yes, it was a miracle. It is also the sixth and seventh steps of AA: (6. Were entirely ready to have God remove all these defects of character. 7. Humbly asked Him to remove our shortcomings). Since that time I have been whole.

Since I was still alive one month later, I was at my first Onsite experience. Now that I was whole I was looking to validate and to solidify my wholeness.

Sharon was concerned about my mental well-being. They hadn't had a M.P.D. go through the experience before and they wanted to have my therapist on standby in case there was a problem. I was so afraid they were going to ask me to leave. I kept telling them, "I'm whole now. I won't split."

They suggested that as I reflected on my past and did my work, I should keep in mind that my one body experienced all of the happenings. I should concentrate on that, rather than which one of my parts experienced the happenings. Since then that suggestion has proved to be a very powerful tool, helping me to feel more at one with myself when working on past issues.

As the Reconstruction process proceeded through the day, I found myself feeling stronger and stronger. It was wonderful to see the healing taking place before my very eyes. All fears of the process were gone. I was ready to dive into this next phase of my recovery. Now I could see why others returned. I knew I couldn't work out all I needed to do in just one session.

Return I did, four workshops and one reunion in two years. You'd think it would become repetitive, not true—each time was completely different and yet equally as exciting as the first. Sometimes I would try to orchestrate the work I wanted to do in group, only to wind up working on an issue I hadn't even considered. Then throughout the various activities of the workshop experience, all of the issues I had been concerned about would be addressed and worked through.

Sometimes playing a part for others' sculpturing would address one of the issues, sometimes they would be addressed as part of the star's work, sometimes just by sharing experiences with others over a meal or breaktime. How could I forget the healing derived via the play times as well as therapy times? It was difficult sometimes to differentiate between the two.

Another interesting phenomenon I found was that the amount of hard work and positive gain I derived from each workshop was directly proportional to the amount of "exciting" challenges and deep-felt experiential pain I would receive not long after my return home.

At my first Reconstruction I took giant steps in awareness, knowledge, perseverance, acceptance and willingness to do emotional discharge work in group. With the support and strength of the group, I was privileged to experience my rebirth. This act opened my eyes to see that it was fear of abandonment and the reality of my mother's rejection and disappointment of me because I was ugly as well as disfigured that set me up to shut down and begin to split. I also learned that I had a choice as to whether or not I would split, just like the alcoholic had a choice about drinking.

Upon returning to my home, I faced up to the reality that I, Kathryn, was not going to live in fear of beatings one more day. My husband calmly said he was not about to be "forced" to work on his anger and moved out, and we were divorced.

I remarried a recovering compulsive gambler, and we attended our second Reconstruction on our honeymoon. We later attended a third workshop with my two daughters and LW's stepson. Over the next few months, LW returned to gambling. I obtained a legal separation to protect the assets from his disease. LW went to a treatment center for co-dependency and gambling. Upon return home he suffered from and almost succumbed to Legionnaire's Disease. He refused, for financial reasons, to be hospitalized and was treated at home by me. Still recovering, LW stole several saleable assets and left me holding the bag for all of the debts. In the midst of all this, I was preparing for my own Reconstruction.

The Reconstruction process was awesome to me. I was thrilled to have been selected. The work I had accomplished to this point had stripped me of all my defense mechanisms, leaving me exposed and raw. I felt the impact of the disease of co-dependency when the last defense of caretaking was removed when LW took off.

I was also fired from one of the top-paying jobs in the area the day before I was to receive a consolidation loan. To add insult to injury, my former employer stated she would not recommend me for a position elsewhere. What a shock to my system. I had always had top evaluations. (We sure do self-destruct under the full power of the disease.) I didn't know what to do next as good jobs were almost impossible to find. In order to hang in there until my Reconstruction, I consciously chose every day not to split and to thank God for my ability to feel the pain from time to time. That was how I knew I wasn't medicating the pain in some self-destructive manner.

I reached South Dakota ready to work and to trust the recovery process! Sharon reviewed my life story with me, then we both in our own ways turned the entire affair over to God. On the day of the Reconstruction it was as if Sharon placed a scalpel in my hand. With the grace of God and the spiritual strength of the group, she directed me to the areas which needed to be cut out. After the day was over, I could not have told you what I had learned, I just knew that I was empty of the painful diseased tumors, raw in the areas of removal and in need of rest and healing. In time the lessons became apparent.

Here is what I gained:

I learned the importance of a good **support system**. At my Reconstruction Sharon had me assemble that first, so I could feed off their strength when the going got rough and/or I would tire.

Abandonment issues, a co-dependent's biggest fear! That is what triggered me to shut down my emotional growth at three days of age and to begin my addiction of M.P.D.

I chose to create my own person to care for, love and comfort me. She did a mighty fine job of it for 40 years. Thus I set up my pattern of survival. If at any time in my life I would experience abandonment or rejection or feel trapped into an ugly situation by the fear of death, beatings or expulsion from a family unit, I would split or create a new person. This was also a way to internalize my anger. If I was rejected just for the way I looked at birth, what would they do if I ever dared to express any negative feelings toward them? Better to chop myself up and allow them to use and abuse all parts of me than to be alone!

Sharon required me to write a list of my rights. It took me two days to come up with 42, one for each year of my life at that time. I was asked to read 12 of them to the group at closing. By the end of the reading I was beginning to believe them. I continued to read them daily for quite some time after returning home. It continued to make a believer out of me with each reading.

When I became whole, my extra people had disappeared in an instant. It was very unsettling for me to reintroduce them as they appeared through my life. My stand-in assumed the various roles for them in order for me to keep them at a safe distance. Through this exercise I was able to validate their former existence with the group at large and to thank them publicly for a job well done. It also allowed me to say my final farewells.

I gained two other insights from that experience.

1. A validation to myself that the work I had done two years ago to be whole was good and complete.
2. It was in my best interest to ONLY use the name Kathryn, not any of the former names as a nickname. Their characteristics were still fresh in my memory banks, and I was still functioning under too much stress.

Another awakening is what actually happened to me as a result of the Reconstruction process. As I implied earlier, it is not a quick fix, nor is it a magical cure, nor is it the final curtain of the recovery process. It did, however, empty me of all of the ugly dysfunctional characteristics of the past. It put an end to the old ways of coping, reacting and behaving, thus allowing me to build on positive characteristics. It also has allowed me to see that I have the ability to make choices for my reactions and behavior. It is a new beginning, one which will make it possible for me to be nurtured and to grow in my recovery on a higher plane.

My life now continues to have its ups and downs, to have good and evil. The myth of living happily ever after is gone, just like my other people are gone. They were all just whiffenpoof dust anyway (totally unrealistic). Now there is a difference as I allow myself to be loved and spoiled (most of the time — steady improvement). I know how to celebrate the good times when they come. And to seek guidance in learning alternative solutions with the challenging times.

The biggest challenge was trying one last time to build a relationship with LW. He relapsed again, began gambling and stole assets of mine and my daughter's. Here came the hardest lesson of all. Just because I love someone and they love me, it does not mean that the relationship is a good one for me.

It was necessary to really trust the process of recovery for quite a while after returning home. The feeling of void lasted for months. Various situations would arise, I knew I couldn't/wouldn't handle them as I had in the past yet I wasn't quite sure how to handle them now. My support system was in service a lot during that time of transition. Then one day the answer was there for me without having to talk to a host of supporters. And much to my surprise, it was a good answer. Just as if I had been doing it that way all along. Now it is a rare case when I need to call for help in my decision-making.

The abandonment issue really challenged me in that first year. Not only did I have to face LW's departure, but my youngest daughter did not return home after visiting her father for part of the summer, the older girl struggled with leaving as well, I lost three members of my support system by their deaths and I experienced harassment with threats of suits, foreclosures and imprisonment on a daily basis for three months. At times I would hop onto my pity-pot. I would look at all I had walked away from in order to obtain and maintain my sanity. Then I would cry out, "The price is too HIGH. It's not worth losing all those people, places and things I had loved and enjoyed."

After some good sobs my new thinking would kick in and I'd be grateful I was feeling the pain which was appropriate for the overwhelming situations. I'd say to myself, "Splitting is not the answer or an option. Hang in there! God has the answer and it is far better than what you have in mind for yourself."

This time I was able to continue working at my new job without distraction from what was going on in my personal life. Needless to say, the income helped to quiet most of the harassment. I let the attorney and the accountant settle the pressing legal problems with the IRS and the bank. A bit more breathing room.

The issue of my daughter's leaving didn't give me a number of choices. I let go and let God, and that has ultimately worked out for the best. Although I lost three dear friends, God gave me six more, including a renewed relationship with my eldest daughter, who is now involved in her own 12-step work. The other five go back a long way too.

After all is said and done, I will most definitely claim that my recovery is worth doing whatever it takes because I am worth it.

More Miracles

The miracle of my life is that I now feel totally connected to myself as well as to God. As a result I feel more open, free, honest and loving in all my relationships. The abundance of energy and of joy is more than I would have ever dreamed possible. I am truly one grateful recovering co-dependent.

Elaine B. Walker
Trustee, Ardine D. &
Bertha H. Walker Foundation

My miracle was that I broke free from the fears taught in my family of origin by trusting and acting on my own truths while losing a mate, friends and the only life I knew. From this came new ways of formulating questions and seeking answers. I have learned to give and receive appropriately and skillfully and the result is miraculous. I learned that when I had the courage to fight for myself that I could affect my world. I now take the truths that enabled me to develop some sense of hope and meaning and teach others how to do the same.

Karen Herrick, CSW, CAC
Founder & Executive Director
Center for Children of Alcoholics, Inc.

I entered recovery as a smashed crayon box — the crayons all twisted, broken, scattered and lost. The miracle of my recovery is freedom: freedom from spiritual bankruptcy, addiction, pride, delusions, despair, anger, fear, shame, doom. Freedom, *one day at a time.*

The "magic fix" that I sought externally, I am discovering within. Instead of seeing myself as diminished and flawed, today I view myself as lovable and worthwhile. I'm becoming my best friend. My health has significantly improved. Today I'm free to live instead of relive, to take risks instead of running or hiding or fighting, to respond instead of reacting. I'm free to investigate my expectations: delusions of timetables, guarantees, power, perfection. I can make choices based on clear perspectives. I'm free to discard those attitudes and behaviors that perpetuate the conditions that cause me pain and shame. I'm free from the unrest of silence.

Today my life is progressively enriched with comfort, enjoyment, serenity and with nurturing people. The price of freedom is accepting that which involves change and a reliance on a power greater than myself.

I'm no longer a victim of my inheritance, my life's experiences or my surroundings. I am FREE. I have CHOICES. I am a miracle. So are *you!*

Kathryn Wade

Divorced three times, alcoholic, suicidal, relationship-dependent . . . I was allergic, had cluster migraines, low back pain and recurrent vaginal cancer. I wanted to die. Recovery has given me life. I have sobriety, am disease-free, relationship-free and my best friends are women. *My* life is now attracting others to recovery — they want the peace and serenity I have. I am *asked* to share my recovery story, my healing and spiritual strength. Where once there was only self-destruction lives a spiritual sparkle spreading life and hope. That's my miracle.

Donna M.

The miracle that I experience is the ability to wake up each day and embrace the little boy I once was. Together the little boy in me and I get together to explore the world and find new adventures to live. The miracle is to be open and feel the new life bubbling out of my being to share with those around me. I am no longer sentenced to die young. I can live young regardless of my age. I am happy to be ALIVE in my feelings. It's a miracle!

RHD, a priest

One of the things I've come to recognize clearly is my unhealthy enmeshment with the lives of my nine brothers and sisters and with my parents. Part of my aftercare has been to let each of them know (in person) that I need a year of no communication with them in order to experience myself as a person separate from them. I have begun, as a result, to clarify my own issues. In the near future I'll be participating weekly in a group therapy process. I anticipate that the guidance and support I'll find there will enable me to move consistently forward in a "new life" direction and to invite others into that gift space.

Jane J.

★

The miracle of my recovery began about 10 years ago with the death of our infant son, Brett. It was the ultimate powerlessness for me. I began to question "Why me, God?" in a very negative, self-pitying way.

Today that has completely turned around. When I ask "Why me, God?" it is asked with tears of joy and gratitude. God has given me many gifts, the most special of which is a "little angel" named Brett who leads me to other "angels" like Sharon. Even more wondrous is that He has given me the ability to go through life with my eyes open and the courage to take the risks necessary for growth and happiness.

Kathy Higby

My inner child shared my history of abuse with me. I listened and believed. With the help of treatment and a new family of choice, I have a voice. I am no longer a lost child. I am releasing the feelings of shame, guilt and fear. I now have a straight back. I've had a curvature for as long as I remember. I had short, stubby finger nails and now have pretty, healthy ones.

I am a growing woman with a special child inside willing to live. I am grateful to God for giving me freedom. My miracle is me.

Mary Ellen R.
Recovering Person

Freedom has to be a truly special miracle. Today I am free to experience my feelings and to share them with those who are important to me. My feelings have set me free to grow. As I take risk each day of my life, I learn a little bit more about who I am. Today I am not so fast to judge others too harshly, and am able to love and nurture myself as my respect for myself and my fellow human beings grow. The process of my recovery is guided by my Higher Power, who continues to set me free to use the gifts that I have been granted. Life is filled with choices, and I have chosen to feel, to grow and to stay free.

Raymond F. Higby, D.O.

As soon as I began taking healthy risks, being able to express what was important for me, and taking action — even when I felt fearful and doubtful — many doors opened in my life. I began a process of healing little by little as I felt "safe." I felt the freedom, love and acceptance that I had searched for most of my life.

Debra E. Moulton
Kingston, MA

There are so many miracles in my recovery that I will name just a few: my love for my alcoholic mother; the relationship I have with my dog; my formation of healthy relationships with men and women who really are there for me; my ability to take care of myself in a thousand ways and to know that the way I take care of myself this afternoon may well be quite different from the way that I need to take care of myself this evening; and my ability to let others take care of themselves.

I believe now that I really do not know what is best for anyone else. The greatest miracle of my recovery is my renewed relationship with God — the deep-seated knowledge that He is always with me, that I am just where I am supposed to be, that I am all right and that He speaks to me personally and through the people in my life. These miracles are wondrous gifts.

Linda M., Ph.D.

The miracle of recovery in my life is being able to be myself, even explore who that is and not worry about what other people think about me. All of my life it seems I did just about everything for some form of approval. Grades, manners, friends, marriage, college, career, all in looking back were for someone else, for their approval. Now I can allow myself to "be" in the cautious, tenuous and vivid manner I want because I am free to be, to know and experience my very own self. The sense of freedom that comes with this release from others is a miracle. And in allowing myself to be myself, I can allow others to be themselves. Each of us has our own Higher Power. It is another miracle that I found mine and me.

Selene and Free

My recovery has indeed been a miracle. To be free from the bondage of my past and my co-dependency issues is a miracle to behold. I am finally free to make the necessary choices in my life.

Lynne Eschbach

The Miracle Continues . . .

Other Books By . . .

HEALTH COMMUNICATIONS, INC.

Enterprise Center
3201 Southwest 15th Street
Deerfield Beach, FL 33442
Phone: 800-851-9100

ADULT CHILDREN OF ALCOHOLICS
Janet Woititz
Over a year on The New York Times Best Seller list,this book is the primer on Adult Children of Alcoholics.
ISBN 0-932194-15-X   **$6.95**

STRUGGLE FOR INTIMACY
Janet Woititz
Another best seller, this book gives insightful advice on learning to love more fully.
ISBN 0-932194-25-7   **$6.95**

DAILY AFFIRMATIONS: For Adult Children of Alcoholics
Rokelle Lerner
These positive affirmations for every day of the year paint a mental picture of your life as you choose it to be.
ISBN 0-932194-27-3   **$6.95**

CHOICEMAKING: For Co-dependents, Adult Children and Spirituality Seekers — Sharon Wegscheider-Cruse
This useful book defines the problems and solves them in a positive way.
ISBN 0-932194-26-5   **$9.95**

LEARNING TO LOVE YOURSELF: Finding Your Self-Worth
Sharon Wegscheider-Cruse
"Self-worth is a choice, not a birthright", says the author as she shows us how we can choose positive self-esteem.
ISBN 0-932194-39-7   **$7.95**

LET GO AND GROW: Recovery for Adult Children
Robert Ackerman
An in-depth study of the different characteristics of adult children of alcoholics with guidelines for recovery.
ISBN 0-932194-51-6   **$8.95**

LOST IN THE SHUFFLE: The Co-dependent Reality
Robert Subby
A look at the unreal rules the co-dependent lives by and the way out of the dis-eased reality.
ISBN 0-932194-45-1   **$8.95**

New Books . . .
from Health Communications

BRADSHAW ON: THE FAMILY: A Revolutionary Way of Self-Discovery
John Bradshaw
The host of the nationally televised series of the same name shows us how families can be healed and we as individuals can realize our full potential.
ISBN 0-932194-54-0   **$9.95**

HEALING THE CHILD WITHIN: Discovery and recovery for Adult Children of Dysfunctional Families — Charles Whitfield
Dr. Whitfield defines, describes and discovers how we can reach our Child Within to heal and nurture our woundedness.
ISBN 0-932194-40-0   **$8.95**

WHISKY'S SONG: An Explicit Story of Surviving in an Alcoholic Home
Mitzi Chandler
A beautiful but brutal story of growing up where violence and neglect are everyday occurrences conveys a positive message of survival and love.
ISBN 0-932194-42-7   **$6.95**

New Books on Spiritual Recovery . . .
from Health Communications

THE JOURNEY WITHIN: A Spiritual Path to Recovery
Ruth Fishel
This book will lead you from your dysfunctional beginnings to the place within where renewal occurs.
ISBN 0-932194-41-9   **$8.95**

LEARNING TO LIVE IN THE NOW: 6-Week Personal Plan To Recovery
Ruth Fishel
The author gently introduces you to the valuable healing tools of meditation, positive creative visualization and affirmations.
ISBN 0-932194-62-1   **$7.95**

GENESIS: Spirituality in Recovery for Co-dependents
by Julie D. Bowden and Herbert L. Gravitz
A self-help spiritual program for adult children of trauma, an in-depth look at "turning it over" and "letting go".
ISBN 0-932194-56-7   **$6.95**

GIFTS FOR PERSONAL GROWTH AND RECOVERY
Wayne Kritsberg
Gifts for healing which include journal writing, breathing, positioning and meditation.
ISBN 0-932194-60-5   **$6.95**

Books from . . .
Health Communications

THIRTY-TWO ELEPHANT REMINDERS: A Book of Healthy Rules
Mary M. McKee
Concise advice by 32 wise elephants whose wit and good humor will also
be appearing in a 12-step calendar and greeting cards.
ISBN 0-932194-59-1 $3.95

BREAKING THE CYCLE OF ADDICTION: For Adult Children of Alcoholics
Patricia O'Gorman and Philip Oliver-Diaz
For parents who were raised in addicted families, this guide teaches you
about Breaking the Cycle of Addiction from *your* parents to your children.
Must reading for any parent.
ISBN 0-932194-37-0 $8.95

AFTER THE TEARS: Reclaiming The Personal Losses of Childhood
Jane Middelton-Moz and Lorie Dwinnel
Your lost childhood must be grieved in order for you to recapture your
self-worth and enjoyment of life. This book will show you how.
ISBN 0-932194-36-2 $7.95

ADULT CHILDREN OF ALCOHOLICS SYNDROME: From Discovery to Recovery
Wayne Kritsberg
Through the Family Integration System and foundations for healing the
wounds of an alcoholic-influenced childhood are laid in this important
book.
ISBN 0-932194-30-3 $7.95

OTHERWISE PERFECT: People and Their Problems with Weight
Mary S. Stuart and Lynnzy Orr
This book deals with all the varieties of eating disorders, from anorexia to
obesity, and how to cope sensibly and successfully.
ISBN 0-932194-57-5 $7.95

Orders must be prepaid by check, money order, MasterCard or Visa.
Purchase orders from agencies accepted (attach P.O. documentation)
for billing. Net 30 days.

Minimum shipping/handling — $1.25 for orders less than $25. For
orders over $25, add 5% of total for shipping and handling. Florida
residents add 5% sales tax.